T0115104

WHY I TAKE
THE BIBLE SERIOUSLY
BUT NOT LITERALLY

Books by Dr. Eugene C. Rollins

Grace Is Not a Blue-Eyed Blonde (Grace is the joyous unmerited blessing of God.)

The Masks We Wear (Wearing a mask may become a subpersonality preventing us from embracing our true spiritual identities.)

The Power of the Spoken Word (Sticks and stones my break my bones, but words will hurt me until the day I die.)

Taming My Tongue (A study guide to recognizing *The Power of the Spoken Word*.)

WHY I TAKE
THE BIBLE SERIOUSLY
BUT NOT LITERALLY

One may study the Bible seriously, respectfully, and
reverently without believing it literally.

Dr. Eugene C. Rollins

authorHOUSE®

AuthorHouse™
1663 Liberty Drive
Bloomington, IN 47403
www.authorhouse.com
Phone: 833-262-8899

Published by AuthorHouse 02/09/2021

ISBN: 978-1-4670-4302-1 (sc)
ISBN: 978-1-4670-4301-4 (hc)
ISBN: 978-1-4670-4303-8 (e)

Library of Congress Control Number: 2013901139

Print information available on the last page.

I dedicate this book to Ms. Toni W. Kelly, office manager of the Liberty Hill Presbyterian Church. She was my office manager, friend, and confidant for six years before I retired from the church in December 2011.

Neither this book nor the past four books would have been possible without her. She has typed and retyped, read and re-read the manuscripts. She has been the contact person with AuthorHouse Publishing and has spared me many of those details.

But more importantly than that, she has run interference for me at the church. This "Summer Series of Sermons" was the most controversial series I have ever preached, and she was there to field many questions before they got to me.

Many thanks, Toni, for work well done!

CONTENTS

INTRODUCTION

ORIGIN OF THE MATERIAL

The origin of the material in these sermons began in 1968. I was a student at Wofford College and pastoring a small mission church in Spartanburg, South Carolina. At that time, there was much unrest in colleges throughout the nation. The Kent State massacre in May of 1970 caused hundreds of student strikes to form at universities and colleges. Wofford's response was to form open discussions with students. The college president, Paul Harding, could often be seen sitting cross-legged upon the grass, talking with students. I ate lunch each day with professors in the school cafeteria, and these conversations were more educational to me than the classes. It was at one of these lunches that my sociology professor said to me, "I can't assign you this reading without assigning it to the entire class, but you will do yourself a great injustice if you do not read *The Age of Reason* by Thomas Paine written in 1794." That was all he needed to say! I read it then and have read it several times in the many years since.

A second experience in seminary also contributed to these sermons. The famous bishop Gerald Kennedy of the United Methodist Church was a visiting speaker. After chapel, I asked him if he had one piece of advice for a young preacher, what it would it be. He responded: "Never read anything you could have written, and never read anything you agree with." These words changed my life! About that time, John A. T. Robinson wrote a book titled *Honest to God*, and many of the students burned it. I had to read it! I have read it many times over the years. With him, I can only say, "All I can do is to try to be honest—and honest about God."

The sermons in this book are a culmination of forty-seven years of struggle trying to be honest about God with God's people. In relationship to the people, I struggle with my dual role as prophet and priest. The prophet confronts the people, and the priest comforts the people. I am to comfort the troubled and trouble the comfortable; these sermons were developed with this dual struggle in mind. The first sermon is from the priest, and the second is from the prophet, and that order continues throughout the series.

In relationship to the Bible, the dual struggle is clear. As the priest, I take the Bible seriously because it changes lives. I have never heard anyone give testimony that reading Plato's *Republic*, Virgil's *Aeneid*, Homer's *Odyssey*, Cicero's *Moral Ethics*, or John Stewart Mill's *Liberty* changed their lives. But thousands of people have given testimony of how reading the Bible has changed their lives forever. As the prophet, I say that no book has been more abused than the Bible or more misunderstood. It has been a playground for lunatics, profit for the charlatans, a profession for the clergy, a problem for theologians, and a puzzle for the general public.

I developed the sermons in this book and delivered them orally. They were delivered to a lakeside congregation of about three hundred people. After I delivered the sermons orally, they were transcribed into written form, and I have tried to maintain the integrity of the spoken word. I use a sermon syllabus format that is fully explained in my book *Grace Is Not a Blue-Eyed Blonde*. A sermon syllabus is included at the beginning of each chapter of this book, and it is the only thing I had with me in the pulpit other than the Bible.

Because of the nature of these sermons, I offered a discussion time after each service for persons who were struggling with anything I said during the sermon.

May God bless you in your struggle in trying to be honest with God, the Bible, and yourself.

Shalom,
Gene Rollins, Author

THOUGHT PROVOKERS

I do not take literally the law that says we should kill all homosexuals.

"If a man has sexual relations with a man as one does with a woman, both of them have done what is detestable. They are to be put to death; their blood will be on their own heads" (Lev. 20:13 NIV).

CHAPTER 1

I Take the Bible Seriously Because It Changes Lives

Sermon Syllabus

Text: 2 Corinthians 5:17; Ephesians 4:20-24

Central Idea of the Text (CIT): Paul taught that the Holy Spirit using the Word of God could change a person into a different person.

Thesis: The Spirit-infused Word of God has the power to change lives today.

Introduction

Outline:
    I. The Words of Jesus Changed Saul into Paul—Acts 9:1-22
    II. The Words of Jesus Changed Zacchaeus the Thieving Tax Collector into a Benevolent Follower—Luke 19:1-10
    III. The Words of Jesus Changed the Unsavory Woman of Samaria into a Witness For Jesus—John 4:1-42
    IV. The Words of Jesus Changed My Life in 1961
    V. The Words of Jesus Can Change Your Life Today!

Conclusion

THE WORD OF THE LORD

2 Corinthians 5:17
"Therefore, if anyone is in Christ, he is a new creation; the old has gone, the new has come!"

Ephesians 4:22-24
"You were taught, with regard to your former way of life, to put off your old self, which is being corrupted by its deceitful desires; to be made new in the attitude of your minds; and to put on the new self, created to be like God in true righteousness and holiness."

INTRODUCTION

I relate to the scriptures reverently, with respect and awe. Contrary to what some people say and believe, the scriptures may be taken seriously and not literally. In fact, I believe one cannot take them both seriously and literally. But this morning, I hope to nail down for you why I take seriously these scriptures.

Around AD 354-430, one of our church fathers, Saint Augustine of Hippo, was in his own words a very sinful person. He wrote in his masterful classic confession about his reprobate life. He was born to a Christian mother and family. He was devoted in early life but greatly strayed in his young adult life. In his search through heathenism, this phrase came to his mind: *pick up and read*. These words continued to rumble around in the hallways of his mind: *pick up and read*. Augustine knew what that meant. He had to read the Word before but as a philosopher and not as a seeker of God. This was the first time he picked up and read the Living Word of God, and it changed his life. *Pick up and read*. And in that reading, Augustine laid off the old self and put on the new self and became one of the most prolific writers of all of our Christian forefathers. I don't agree with all that he said, but he was a masterful writer and in his day a defender of the scripture.

I. THE WORDS OF JESUS CHANGED SAUL INTO PAUL—ACTS 9:1-22

Paul writes and says that these words have the ability to create a new creation. These words, infused by the Holy Spirit, made alive by the Spirit of God, have the power to lay off an old self and put on a new self.

There are marvelous works of literature in this world, but how many of you have heard someone say, "I read Shakespeare's *Hamlet* or Shakespeare's *Julius Caesar*, and my life was changed! I read about Romeo and Juliet from Shakespeare's work, and my life has just been radically altered, and I am filled with the love Shakespeare speaks about"? Have you ever heard a testimony like that? I have not. The world is filled with great literature, but have you heard anyone say, "You know, I was reading *Moby Dick*, that marvelous tale of a fish, and that fish walked out of that story into my life, and it has never been the same"? Have you?

The man who wrote those words was a Pharisee, a Jew, a member of the Sanhedrin, and one of the most devout men of his day, and when this little group of people called "The Way"—and that is what Christians were first called, people of "The Way"—Paul felt Judaism was under attack, and he personally committed himself to stomp out the little religious sect called the people of "The Way." Outside the walls of Jerusalem, Paul encouraged the stoning of Steven and even held the cloaks of those who threw the stones that killed this brilliant young man. Paul went throughout Jerusalem incarcerating, confiscating the property of, and locking up men and women because they were people of "The Way." He did so well that he received from the Sanhedrin and the high priest papers to move out of Jerusalem and go into Damascus to do the same.

And while he was on the road to Damascus, a brilliant light knocked him to the ground, and he heard this voice: "Saul, why are you persecuting me?" And Paul said, "Who are you? I am persecuting these people called the people of 'The Way.' Who are you?" And Jesus said, "I am Jesus." And I know Paul had this thought race down his mind: *But he is dead. We killed him and entombed him, and they created this miracle story about him coming out and hid his body somewhere.* And then Jesus said to Paul, who was then called Saul of Tarsus, "Has it been difficult for you to ward off those pangs of conscience?"

"Has it been difficult for you" in the King James translation is a little confusing; it is a "kick against the Pricks"; the Greek word is *gourds*. Those

3

stakes that have been sticking in your conscience. Immediately Paul knew what He was talking about, and Paul said, "What do you want of me?" And there the greatest Christian missionary, the most zealous Christian missionary that was ever given breath, was born that day on the road to Damascus. The words of Jesus became alive in his life, and he was changed from a persecutor of "The Way" to a proclaimer of "The Way."

II. THE WORDS OF JESUS CHANGED ZACCHAEUS THE THIEVING TAX COLLECTOR INTO A BENEVOLENT FOLLOWER—LUKE 19:1-10

Plato's *The Republic* is a marvelous work. But I have never heard anyone say, "I was reading Plato's *The Republic*, and I became so convinced that I was moving in the wrong direction from reading that book that I changed and went in a different direction. You know, I got enough power from Plato's words and Plato's book *The Republic* that my life has never ever been the same." I have never heard that.

Once again last year I read *The Epic of Gilgamesh*, which is fifteen hundred years older than the Noah story. It is a marvelous work, a work of antiquity, but I have never heard anyone say, "Wow, that *Epic of Gilgamesh* is so powerful that I was reading it and something happened to me, and my heart and life changed in such a way that it has never been the same." I have never heard that.

In Jesus's day, for sixty years the Roman government had occupied Jerusalem, and they had levied some horribly high taxes upon the citizens of Jerusalem, and some of the citizenry became tax collectors for their own people. Zacchaeus was one of those people. The scriptures tell us in Luke chapter 19 that Zacchaeus was rich. You do not make enough money collecting taxes to become rich. Zacchaeus had his finger in the pie. It was bad enough that he was a tax collector for his own people. He was despised, scorned, and rejected, and this rich little man had a longing in his heart, and he ran up a road in Jericho upon which he heard Jesus was traveling. Being so little in stature and knowing he could not elbow his way through the crowd, he climbed up in a sycamore tree very much like our little water oaks. And as he waited up in this tree, waiting for Jesus to come down the road, we know not what kind of questions he had, but Jesus stopped and looked up and said, "Zacchaeus, get out of that tree. I am going to spend the day at your house." Zacchaeus said, "Lord, half of everything I have I am going to give to the poor. Half of it. And if I have taken anything illegally, I am going to return four times." According to Leviticus, the law said he had to give what he had taken plus one-fifth. Zacchaeus said, "I will return it fourfold whatever I have taken illegally." What changed him? The words of Jesus changed him.

I don't know if you remember reading that masterful work *Aeneid* by Virgil. I do, but I have never heard anyone say, "I was reading that tale of antiquity, and something gripped me, and I became an entirely different individual." There are many other works that are marvelous. For example, John Stewart Mills's work on liberty and Cicero's marvelous work on moral ethics. I have never heard anyone say, "You know, I was a thief, and I read Cicero's moral ethics, and my life took a different direction. I quit stealing, and I started returning fourfold to people I had taken things from." They are marvelous works of literature, but I never have heard one testimony as to how these marvelous works of antiquity, beautiful and powerful though they are, inspired anyone to say, "Oh, my life has been radically altered."

III. THE WORDS OF JESUS CHANGED THE UNSAVORY WOMAN OF SAMARIA INTO A WITNESS FOR JESUS—JOHN 4:1-42

Jesus was on His way, and He took a detour into Samaria, a forbidden land for a Jew. His disciples went into a nearby town, and He was at the well at Sycars. A woman came up to Him, and He asked for a drink of water. She was astonished that this Jew would speak to a Samarian. She was astonished at the second point that this male Jew would speak to a female Samarian. They began a dialogue, and in that dialogue, Jesus said to her, "Run home and fetch your husband. Come back. I would like to talk to both of you." And she said, "I have no husband." And Jesus said, "You are absolutely honest, but you have had five. And the man you are now living with is not your husband." And she was like, "Wow, you must be a prophet." And Jesus talked to her and finally said to her, "True worship is worship in spirit and in truth, for God is spirit." And she left Him and went into the town, telling everyone, "You must come meet this man who just told me everything I have ever done in my life and said it noncondemningly." And her life was set free.

She had been at the well at noon. Women did not go to the well at noon; they went early in the morning when it was cool and late in the evening when it was cool. She went in the heat of the midday sun because she had been rejected, alienated, and scorned, and now she was set free. I have never heard anyone say they read Homer's *Odyssey* and their lives were set free, liberated, forgiven. Never have! That is why I take these words seriously.

IV. THE WORDS OF JESUS CHANGED MY LIFE IN 1961

I did not grow up in a church. My father was a deacon in a Freewill Baptist Church when he died at age forty-two. I was age four. We never went back to church again after that. At age eighteen, I married the girl I had impregnated. At twenty-one, we had two children and another one on the way. At that point and time, I wasn't all that horrible of a person, but I had been. And I came down with the mumps.

I was in the retail food business, and I remember the man who gave them to me, one of my customers. The doctor scared the daylights out of me when he described what could happen to a male if the mumps fell. He said, "Go home and go to bed," and I went home and went to bed. The children were in the nursery, the wife was working, and I was alone. It was the first time I had ever been still in my life. I thought I would go crazy. I read every *Field and Stream* and every *Gun Digest* I had in the house, and the thing that was deeply, deeply pressing my spirit was that I was trying to be a husband and didn't know how to be one. That had not been modeled for me. I was trying to be a father, and that had not been modeled for me. I felt this deep psychological stress as to how to perform these functions that life had placed upon me.

I remember getting my wife's Bible (the Gideons had given it to her when she graduated high school), and I started reading it. All the Zane Grey books I had ever read, I read from front to back, and that was pretty much all I had ever read to that point. I couldn't make head or tails of what was being said, so I started skipping around, you know, like over in the book of Psalms and the book of Job, and they didn't make any sense either. Finally I got over to St. Matthew, and it didn't make a whole lot of sense either. St. Luke couldn't help, but I began to wonder why these two people had the same first names. Then I started reading the book of

John, and God walked out of that book and into my life, and it has not ever been the same, ever. By that I do not mean that my life has been together ever since that day. Not at all. I have been a struggler all my life. But that day radically altered my perspective of who I was, my perspective of what life was, and my perspective of who God was, and that has never changed.

James Robison had a crusade in Dayton, Ohio, a number of years ago. He is from Texas. I knew him in seminary. Two or three days after the revival, a woman looked out of the picture window in her living room and saw a ragged old pickup truck back down her driveway. She went outside, and a man got out of the pickup and started unloading stuff. She recognized that it was all of her pool furniture that had been stolen last year, and the man said to her, "I stole your pool furniture last year, but I have met Jesus, and I want to bring it back to you, and if there is anything else I can do, I want to do it for you." You ever heard of that happening from someone who read the *Gettysburg Address* by Abe Lincoln?

V. THE WORDS OF JESUS CAN CHANGE YOUR LIFE TODAY!

One person made a commitment of faith, and the next week at work, one of his co-workers was chiding him, and the co-worker said, "Do you tell me you believe Jesus turned that water into wine?" And the man said, "I don't know about that, but I know at my house He has turned beer into food and beer into furniture. I don't know about that wine story, but I know what has happened here. I know what has happened in my life and in my home." Is there another book that changes lives like that? No. Point it out to me. Show it to me. Read me the stories. I have never heard them.

In 1891 there was a National League baseball player who had lost everything. He had drunk his way from being number one on his way to the Hall of Fame to a soup kitchen without a dime in his pocket. All he owned was the rags he had on. And one day in 1981, Billy Sunday listened in that soup kitchen as someone took up the Bible and began to read, and in the reading and in the hearing, God walked out of that book into Billy Sunday's life, and he never took another drink. God walked out of that book into his heart and life, and he became the fire brand for the second wave of American revivalism. God walked out of that book into his life, and he set up such an organization that a man later came and used the identical preparatory organization that Billy Sunday set up, and Billy Graham became one of the greatest revivalists of our world.

CONCLUSION

Nothing in the history of humankind has those testimonies. That is why I take this book seriously, and I unapologetically say to you today that if you are willing, the Spirit of God that is infused in this book will walk out of this book into your life, and it will never be the same, ever. Beyond and above everything else, I say this summer do not forget that I have given my life to the preaching of this book primarily because of the changes I have seen, witnessed, felt in my own experience, and seen in the lives of hundreds throughout these forty-six years. Let us pray.

Lord, Your word tells us that in You we become a new creation. If there are those who here this morning or who will be here this summer who have not tasted the newness of that creation, through these days may they find the truth and the reality of Your power to change. May it be so in Jesus's name. Amen.

THOUGHT PROVOKERS

I do not take literally the law that says people who commit adultery should be stoned to death.

"If a man is found sleeping with another man's wife, both the man who slept with her and the woman must die. You must purge the evil from Israel" (Deut. 22:22 NIV).

CHAPTER 2

I Do Not Take the Bible Literally When It Has God Causing Catastrophes

SERMON SYLLABUS

Text: Luke 13:1-5; Job 16:11-17

CIT: Job blamed God for his suffering, but Jesus said suffering comes to us all.

Thesis: We live after the eighteenth-century enlightenment period and no longer need to blame God for everything.

Purpose:
- Major Objective: Doctrinal
- Specific Objective: Through the power of the Holy Spirit, I hope to lead each of us in becoming more responsible for our own actions and the events of our world.

Introduction

Outline:
    I.   The Suffering of Job Caused by God?—Luke 13:1-3
    II. The Death of the Galileans Caused by God?—Luke 13:1-3
    III. The Death of the Workers Caused by God?—Luke 13:4-5

Conclusion

THE WORD OF THE LORD

Luke 13:1-5

> Now there were some present at that time who told Jesus about the Galileans whose blood Pilate had mixed with their sacrifices. Jesus answered, "Do you think that these Galileans were worse sinners than all the other Galileans because they suffered this way? I tell you, no! But unless you repent, you too will all perish. Or those eighteen who died when the tower in Siloam fell on them—do you think they were more guilty than all the others living in Jerusalem? I tell you, no! But unless you repent, you too will all perish."

Job 16:11-17

> God has turned me over to the ungodly and thrown me into the clutches of the wicked. All was well with me, but he shattered me; he seized me by the neck and crushed me. He has made me his target; his archers surround me. Without pity, he pierces my kidneys and spills my gall on the ground. Again and again he bursts upon me; he rushes at me like a warrior. I have sewed sackcloth over my skin and buried my brow in the dust. My face is red with weeping, dark shadows ring my eyes; yet my hands have been free of violence and my prayer is pure.

INTRODUCTION

King Charles II, whose father was beheaded by the Puritans, visited the blind poet John Milton, and King Charles said to Milton, "Your blindness is God's judgment upon you for taking part in my father's death." And Milton looked at the king and said, "God's judgment is upon me and caused my blindness? What say you about the death of your father?"[1] Is it not interesting how we use our theology almost always for our own betterment? On March 11, 2011, an earthquake measuring 9.0 on the Richter scale hit Japan. Thirteen thousand were killed, three thousand were injured, and fifteen thousand were unaccounted for, and I have been waiting for one of our theologians in America to say that the earthquake hit Japan because of Pearl Harbor. I have been amazed that I have not heard it. Maybe it has been said, and it just didn't get to me.

In 2004, the worst tsunami history has ever recorded hit Indonesian. Two hundred and thirty thousand people were killed. It was the worst in history, and they have been recording tsunamis since 426 BC. It is amazing to me that in 426 BC, a Greek mathematician posed the theory that a tsunami wave was caused by an underocean earthquake. Is that not something? In 426 BC?

I was walking with a friend on the beach just a few days after the 2004 tsunami. This friend happens to be Catholic, and as we were watching the beach and watching the waves, the subject of the tsunami came up. And I said to him, "How do you reconcile God in this?" He said, "It was God's will." Just like that. And I said, "It was God's will to kill 230,000 people in one of the poorest continents in the world?" He said, "Yes. Nothing happens without it being God's will." And I said, "Well, how do you reconcile that?" And he said, "I don't reconcile it. It just is." And I thought that Christopher Hitchens and Sam Harris, known atheists, are correct. Our faith is a sacred cow, and we will not bring one ounce of reasoning to it, not one ounce. That was just what he was saying to me. It just is. I don't reconcile that. I don't go there. I don't deal with that. It just is. God's will, pure and simple.

Folks, we live beyond the eighteenth-century enlightenment. We know where tsunamis come from. They don't come from God. We know where earthquakes come from; we know where tornadoes come from; we know where hurricanes come from. God doesn't have anything to do with them. They are 100 percent cosmic physics, nothing else.

I. The Suffering of Job Caused by God?—Luke 13:1-3

In this passage, Job is in God's face. Whoever coined the phrase "the patience of Job" never read the book of Job. Never. There is nothing patient about Job. Nine times in this appointed text he is right in God's face, so he is not patient. But if the book of Job is literal, we really have problems.

God looked at Job while conversing with the devil, and God said to the devil, "Have you considered my servant Job?" Job was perfect, upright, and everything. Well, you know what that tells me right up front? Don't be a good boy. If you are a good boy, God will sic somebody on you. So I am not going to try to be good. No, I am going to spread my wings. So that begins to be problematic for me in the beginning of the book of Job.

Then Job's children are killed. What did they do? Why kill all his children? You see the problematic God in that situation? We know now, those of us who are honest, that the book of Job was written in Iraq. It was written as a play, a drama. When Israel went to Iraq as captives in 586 BC, they were exposed to the drama of Job, and this play tried to get at the cultural problem of Psalm 1, which says if you do good and be good, wonderful things will happen to you. If you don't love God and be good, horrible things will happen to you. And David himself cried out to that. Why do the wicked prosper and the righteous suffer? David saw something wrong with that. So this drama was created out of the Iraqi culture to speak to this, and Israel was exposed to it, liked it, and brought it home when they returned to Israel. But they did not like the ending, so they changed it.

In the drama, during Job's last dialogue with God, God basically said to Job, "Your mind is so puny that you can't understand the works of God. Forget about suffering and evil. You can't understand it." And the play ends. Well, Israel could not handle that, so they had Job having more beautiful children than he had before, more crops, more animals, more gold, more everything than he had before because they could not get away from that idea that if you are good, wonderful things happen to you and if you are bad, horrible things happen to you. Folks, that is just not life. So Job was not a historical person. Job originated as a play, as a drama to speak to this inconsistency of life's experience. So is Job blaming God? You bet. But is it on-target? Absolutely not.

The last case I worked at Richland Memorial Hospital was with a military family whose ten-year-old son had a little ten-year-old buddy over visiting. Their son had taken out his father's military .45 model 1911. A round was in the chamber, and its magazine was full. They took the magazine out; the little boy had that much sense. His little buddy was playing with the gun and shot the boy just between the eyes at a range of about three feet. I was in the emergency room, dealing with this mother whose son had just been shot, and she said to me, "I can't understand why God took my little baby."

Now, above everything else, I am a pastor. In those situations, I don't care about orthodoxy. I am pastor. I said to her, "We do not understand the tragedies of suffering and death." What I wanted to say to her with every fiber of my being was three things: (1) your husband did not have that weapon put away, and he is military, and he should have known better; (2) not only did he not have it put up, but he had one in the chamber, and he should have known better; and (3) your son was ten years old, and your husband should have taught the boy about the weapon, how to use it, what it would do, and what to expect if there was going to be a weapon around the house. I wanted to say to her that God had nothing to do with the death of her son; her husband did. That was the truth. But I would not do that because I was a pastor with her. But that was the truth. God does not orchestrate these tragedies. When we will stop saying, "Why? I don't know why God took my baby." We excuse ourselves from our own stupidity. We excuse ourselves from our own errors, and we lay it at the feet of God, and it is time, folks, that we just quit that.

A client came to me (I am a counselor 2 days a week). His twelve-year-old son had been with the Boy Scouts in the mountains on a bicycle ride and had a heart attack. Twelve years old. They rushed him to the hospital out of those mountains, but he died. The father did not come to me until after the funeral; he came because his Presbyterian preacher said, "God has picked another young beautiful flower for God's garden." The father said to me, "I can't accept that." And I said, "You shouldn't. Your minister was wrong. If that is the kind of God we have, one who reaches down and picks up little twelve-year-olds for some satisfaction that He might have in His garden, I want nothing to do with that kind of God. The child died of a heart attack."

It was tragic. It was sad. But it is time we stop saying, "God took my loved one," and say, "God received my loved one." I know why we say that. I work with suffering every day. It helps us deal with our loss when we say it was his time to go or that God called her home. Then there is a reason for her death, there is a reason for his death, there is an understanding, there is an excuse. But we have other ways to understand that. Disease carried him to God, and God received him.

Just last week, a client coming from Columbia and headed to Lancaster, coming from her boyfriend's home outside of Great Falls, was hit head-on by a drunk person. I don't know how she survived that accident. God's will? Cute little girl, you just did not receive enough punishment lately, so I am going to use this drunk as an instrument and plow directly into the front of your car and see if I can't upset your life just a little bit. God looked down and said, "You know, All State is making too much money. These other places make too much money. I am going to rain a little hell down on Kershaw and cause some of these insurance companies to pay out some money." You see what we do? Absolutely ridiculous. Our cosmic forces are laws of physics. Death is a result of disease, accidents, and tragedies. God does not orchestrate them.

During 9/11, Jerry Falwell said on national television, "It is the feminists, the lesbians, the gays, the homosexuals, and the ACLU who have caused God to touch us with this horrible tragedy." (September 13, 2001 telecast of the 700 Club) Does it matter that he got so much harassment that he withdrew the statement two days later? It does not matter to me. That is what he believes. That is exactly what he believes. Pat Robinson said when they had that horrible earthquake in Haiti that it was God getting back at those poor people for a voodoo pact made two hundred years ago with the devil.[1] What kind of reasoning is all of this? Even the beloved Billy Graham, when JFK Jr. died in that airplane wreck, said on national television, speaking to the Kennedy family, "God took your son." That is a quote. He continued, "But your family has suffered tragedy after tragedy. If you will turn yourself to God's mercy, God will get you through this hard time." (Larry King Live, CNN, July 20, 1999)

Now, you can do that with a conscious mind but not with the unconscious mind. I know you cannot do that. Because the unconscious mind is saying, "Does not compute." I cannot be comforted by the one who just killed my son. We know why JFK died. He put himself in a situation that he was not trained or prepared to deal with. He could not fly a plane with instruments. He flew a plane by sight, and he lost his sight. That is what killed him.

II. The Death of the Galileans Caused by God?—Luke 13:1-3

Jesus uses two wonderful examples. His disciples come to Him and they say, "Lord, this group of Galileans that Pilot moved into, and just while they were offering their sacrifices to God in the outer court of the temple, his soldiers went in and just hacked them up and mixed their blood with the blood of their sacrifices." Just horrible. And Jesus said, "Do you think those men were more horrible than the average Joe Gentile in Galilea? I tell you no." We all suffer like that.

III. The Death of the Workers Caused by God?—Luke 13:4-5

Then He uses His own illustration, one with which they were familiar. He said, "Those workers Pilot enslaved to build that aqueduct had an old guard tower fall on eighteen of them and kill them. Do you think they were so horrible? Not at all. You too will suffer like that." He said. Suffering and death are part of our lives. Let me encourage you to look more responsibly at your own life. I know how you long for comfort in those times of death. I have lost loved ones as well. And I thank God as I look back on my mother's death that I never had anyone say to me, "Well, Gene, you just have to take this because you know it is God's will, and she is so much better off." I would have hit them. I know what killed Mama; her heart killed her. I don't put that at God's feet. I spent enough years in that kind of anger and that kind of reasoning. It is better for us to say, "God did not take my loved ones. God received my loved ones in mercy and in grace."

Conclusion

If you have not read *The Shack,* written by Paul Young, you owe it to yourself. The best statement in the book was when as God's mouthpiece this big black woman speaking for God says, "Just because we bring marvelous, marvelous healing and understandings and everything else out of tragedy, do not believe that we created the tragedy that we bring the good out of."[2] It is the best line in the book. You owe it to yourself to read it.

Let us pray. Jesus, thank You for these two illustrations. Thank You also for that encounter with Your disciples when they said to You, "Here is a man born blind. Did he sin while he was in the womb, or was it his parents' sin?" And Jesus said, "Neither. He is blind." Just as simple as that. Help us, O Lord, in our tragedies to not blame but to trust. Help us not to credit You with the deed but turn to You for Your mercy and Your grace in our horrible times of suffering and loss. May it be so in Jesus's name. Amen.

NOTES

1. Martin Thielen, *What's The Least I Can Believe and Still Be A Christian?* (Louisville: Westminster John Knox Press, 2011), 4-5.
2. William P. Young, *The Shack: A Novel* (Newday Park, CA: Wind Blown Media, 2007), 185.

THOUGHT PROVOKERS

I do not take literally the law that says a child born out of wedlock cannot worship in a congregation.

"No one born of a forbidden marriage nor any of their descendants may enter the assembly of the Lord, not even in the tenth generation" (Deut. 23:2 NIV).

CHAPTER 3

I TAKE SERIOUSLY THE
INSPIRATION OF THE BIBLE

SERMON SYLLABUS

Text: 2 Timothy 3:14-17; 2 Peter 1:19-21

CIT: Paul assured Timothy of the trustworthiness of the scripture.

Thesis: The Bible as we have it today is trustworthy.

Purpose:
- Major Objective: Doctrinal
- Specific Objective: Through the power of the Holy Spirit, I hope to lead each of us in trusting God's Word.

Introduction

Outline:
I. What Is Inspired?—2 Timothy 3:16
   a. To Paul and Peter It Was the Old Testament
   b. To Us Today It May Mean the Old and New Testaments.

II. What Does Inspired Mean?—2 Timothy 3:16; 2 Peter 1:21
   a. Inspiration Is All Human
   b. Inspiration Is All Divine
   c. Inspiration Is Both Human and Divine—Luke 1:1-4

III. What Inspiration Means Is Trust!—2 Peter 1:20-21
   a. The Manuscripts Are Trustworthy
   b. The Versions Are Trustworthy

Conclusion

THE WORD OF THE LORD

2 Timothy 3:14-17

> But as for you, continue in what you have learned and have become convinced of, because you know those from whom you learned it, and how from infancy you have known the Holy Scriptures, which are able to make you wise for salvation through faith in Christ Jesus. All Scripture is God-breathed and is useful for teaching, rebuking, correcting and training in righteousness, so that the servant of God may be thoroughly equipped for every good work.

2 Peter 1:19-21

> We also have the prophetic message as something completely reliable, and you will do well to pay attention to it, as to a light shining in a dark place, until the day dawns and the morning star rises in your hearts. Above all, you must understand that no prophecy of Scripture came about by the prophet's own interpretation of things. For prophecy never had its origin in the human will, but prophets, though human, spoke from God as they were carried along by the Holy Spirit.

INTRODUCTION

Last week when I was in dialogue with a minister, he said to me, "If I can't believe it all, I can't believe any of it." And I said to him, "Well, I believe it all." I believe it all as it is interpreted. I do not believe it literally. I believe all of the scriptures as they are interpreted.

Then the dialogue led us into the sermon teaser that we had put in the bulletin from chapter 10 of Joshua. In chapter 10 of Joshua, Joshua prayed while in a battle, and he prayed and asked God to let the sun stand still for a day and he would win the battle. The scriptures tell us that the sun and the moon stood still for a day.

I said to the minister, "You cannot take that literally, because the sun does not move." It never has. When I stand on my dock in the evening, it is my experience that the sun is moving. In fact, one of my granddaughters says, "Bye." There is nothing about our experience that says the Earth that we are standing on is moving. It is the sun that is going down. It is not the Earth that is turning. He understood that. But then he said, "How do you interpret that passage? You don't take it literally?" I said, "Of course not." He said, "Well, how do you interpret it?" I said, "The interpretation for me . . ." And then immediately in the conversation I was carried back to a former pastorate with a former church member.

This man had bought his son a relatively new Volkswagen for graduation. The week of graduation, his son and three passengers wrapped that Volkswagen around a telephone pole. I met the family in the ER at about 1:00 or 1:30 in the morning and sat with them until the doctor came out about 4:00 a.m. and asked me to come out and talk with him. I had to go back in and tell my parishioners that hospital staff did everything they could but their son died from massive brain injuries. Well, of course all chaos broke loose. It was so hard.

I stayed with the family until 4:00 that afternoon. The father who had purchased the Volkswagen for his now-dead son said to me, "Will this day ever end?" And I said to him, "Yes, it will end, and God will see you through it until the end." You have had those days in your life, and so have I, where either they were so joyous or so horrendously miserable that you thought they would never end. It just seemed that this day would go on forever and that the sun was standing still in the sky.

And I said to my minister friend, "That is how I interpret that text." I interpret that Joshua prayed, and God answered that prayer with a victory but with the sense among them that everything stood still as they fought the horrendous battle. I do take all scripture seriously. I do believe it all. And in this conversation, the minister said to me, "The scripture says all scripture is inspired." And I said, "Yes, it does." And I believe that all scripture is inspired.

I. WHAT IS INSPIRED?—2 TIMOTHY 3:16

Theopneustos means "God" and "breathe," so our translation has it very, very correct that inspiration is God breathing and giving influence, giving guidance upon an individual in a certain situation. But now let us be honest about what 2 Timothy 3:16 says.

In 2 Peter and in 2 Timothy, Timothy and all of Paul's letters were written between AD 60, AD 65, and AD 70. They were the first written material in our New Testament. Just because Matthew is there first doesn't mean Matthew was written first. That is not the way it works. The Epistles of Paul, including Timothy, were written somewhere around AD 55-60, right in there. Mark was not written until AD 65. Matthew and Luke were not written until AD 80-85. John was not written until AD 95-105. And Peter was not written until about AD 120. So when Timothy says, "All scripture is inspired," what it is referring to is the Old Testament, not the New Testament.

The New Testament was not in existence, so when Paul and Peter both said all scripture is inspired, they were talking about the Old Testament. Did you not catch it when Paul said to Timothy, "You have studied the scriptures since infancy." The Holy Scriptures. What scriptures? Well, it has to be the Old Testament. It can't be anything else because nothing else existed at the time. Are you with me? So, we need to be honest about that. When we say "all scripture," we mean that what the Bible is talking about is all of the Old Testament. Now then, that was what Paul and Peter meant. If we want to believe that the New Testament as we have it today is also God-breathed and God-inspired, and I do, we believe God influenced the individuals as they wrote it. I believe that. But let's be honest. You cannot take this text and say that it means that. It does not mean that. It refers to the Old Testament and the Old Testament only because the New Testament was not in existence. So we just need to be clear about that. If you want to believe, and I do, that the New Testament is also inspired. I believe God influenced the writers of the New Testament to put down what they wrote.

That is what Paul means when he says in this passage that it is inspired. What does inspiration mean? I have just defined it for you from Webster and the Greek word. Is inspiration all human? There are those who believe that. I personally do not. But there are those who say Shakespeare was inspired and Plato was inspired, and many of these other works of antiquity were inspired. You have left musicals saying, "That was so inspiring." You have left speeches and said they were so inspiring. Well, there are those who say the Bible is just like that. Humans wrote it. It is a human book, and it is all human. That is it.

While I was a student at Wofford College, there was a professor in the Sociology Department, Dr. Charles Bailey, who I really enjoyed, and apparently he enjoyed some of my antics because he would pick on me often. One day in class, we were studying the social change in a speech of Martin Luther King Jr., and he said to me, "Rollins, do you think that speech was inspired?" And I said, "Absolutely. It is a masterpiece, beautifully constructed, beautifully put together, and magnificently delivered." He said, "So you think it was inspired." I said, "Yes, absolutely." He said, "Do you think it should be included in the canon of scripture?" I said, "No." He said, "Well, if it is inspired, do you think it is inspired of God?" I said, "Yes." He said, "Why shouldn't it be included in the canon?" I said, "The canon is closed." He said, "Who closed it?" I said, "The church." He said, "Who gave them that authority?" I said, "God." He said, "You are treading on thin ice."

II. WHAT DOES INSPIRED MEAN?—2 TIMOTHY 3:16; 2 PETER 1:21

And then there are those who take the other position. The scriptures are divinely inspired, and it is all divine; it is all God. I don't believe that either. I won't get technical and get into all the nomenclature of the theological terms. But one of the phrases you will hear is the *dictation theory*, which means that God simply dictated it word for word. Those who usually take this position say that if we had the original manuscripts, they would give testimony to the dictation. Well, that is a good argument because we don't have any original manuscript. But how can you prove that hypothesis? You cannot.

Our book, I believe, is not all divine. We did not get it from heaven, dropped down on golden plates as is claimed for the Book of Mormon. We did not get it like the Koran; Mohammed claimed that God dictated it to him or, excuse me, an angel did in the desert mountains. He came home and shared it with his family, and they memorized it, and after some years they started writing it down, and it became the Koran. That is not our history. This book is not all human, and it is not all divine; it is both human and divine. God took the human instrument and inspired and infused that human instrument to put down the scriptures. Did God dictate them? Not at all. God inspired them.

If you want proof of that, go to the first chapter of Luke and look at the first four verses of the Gospel of Luke. Luke says in the first four verses, "There have been others [I am paraphrasing] who have put together a history of our faith, but after serious consideration I decided to put down in logical order the stories of our faith." So Luke is just saying that he made a choice to gather the stories that he had heard and look at the stories that had already been written, and he made the choice to write them down. So we see the human instrument in that.

When you go to a Greek class as a student, the Gospel you study is the Gospel of John because it is absolutely perfect in Greek. There is not one error in the whole book. The phrases and clauses are simple. They are simple declarative sentences, and that is where the Greek student starts. It is beautiful Greek. But the same person who wrote the Gospel of John probably could not have written Revelation unless there was some secretarial help somewhere, because the book of Revelation is horrible in its Greek. There are all kinds of mistakes—run-on sentences, incorrect clauses, and horrible grammar.

And then when you go to Peter, our text here, Peter's letters are just about on a third-grade level when it comes to syntax, sentence structure, and grammar. We believe Peter the fisherman wrote the book of Peter; well, if he did, he knew how to fish, but he didn't know Greek grammar and the Greek language rules. So if God was dictating, then why would God not stamp out these errors and make them perfect? God takes a human instrument and uses that human instrument to convey God's Word, God's truth to us today. It is not all human; it is not all divine. It is both human and divine.

III. What Inspiration Means Is Trust!—2 Peter 1:20-21

For me, the basic meaning of inspiration is this: it is trustworthy. We can trust the scriptures that we have to convey to us what God wants conveyed to us. We have about a quarter of a million pieces of manuscripts and full manuscripts of our scriptures. Granted, we do not have the originals, and that upsets some people. But because the parchments were so fragile and they made copies so quickly because they knew they were fragile, what we have are copies. We do not have an original. But we have a quarter of a million, and in 1946 when the Dead Sea Scrolls were unearthed, it gave radical testimony to the accuracy of the scriptures we already had in hand.

So I want to say to us today, and you have heard me critique it and analyze it and everything else, is that I trust it. I trust it to give me guidance, to give me instruction, to give me comfort, to give me encouragement, I trust the scriptures because they change lives. They change and enhance and strengthen lives. I see it every day. And one of the things I see when I work with sick people two days a week is that when I see a Bible that is falling apart, the owner is not. When I see a Bible that is falling apart, I do not find that person's life falling apart. There is something about these words infused by the Holy Spirit that makes a difference in our lives. Granted, it is the most owned book in the world. It is still the highest selling of any book in the world, but according to the latest Gallup polls, while it may be the most revered, it is the least read of any book on the market today.[1]

Back to the conversation I mentioned in the beginning of the sermon. My minister friend and I were funning with each other a little bit, and I said to him, "Do you take literally that God helps those who help themselves?" And he said, "Absolutely." I said, "That is not the Bible. Ben Franklin said that."[2] And I could tell he just wanted to slap the little smart aleck. My mama used to quote that all the time. She thought it was from the Bible. The other one she used to quote was, "Cleanliness is next to Godliness."[3] She didn't know it was not in the Bible.

We can trust the manuscripts if we read them. We can trust even the versions we have today, and there are many, but the Greek scholars Westcott and Hort tell us that all of the manuscripts and versions we have are 99 percent accurate.[4] We do not have one serious doctrine that rests on a questionable text. Not one. There are lots of differences, but not one major doctrine is in conflict because of the manuscripts or the versions and the different translations.

The infidel and atheist Voltaire said, "Within a hundred years of my death the only Bible that will exist will be in a museum. Christianity is in its twilight years." He said that before he died in 1788. One hundred years after he made that prophecy from his house, the Geneva Bible Convention owned his house and occupied it. On that same day, his latest work sold in Paris for 11 cents.[5] On that same day in1888, $500,000 was paid to a Russian czar for the *Codex Sinaiticus* manuscript. It is the first full manuscript we have. It had been put in a monastery in AD 367, and it was found there and sold for $500,000 on the very day Voltaire's book sold for 11 cents.[4] The scriptures told us in the beginning in Isaiah's prophecy that the grass will wither and the flowers will fade but this book will outlast the world (Isa. 40:8), and I believe it.

CONCLUSION

Sir Walter Raleigh was on his death bed—aged, infirmed, dying—and he said to his son-in-law Lockhart, "Son, go get me the book." Sir Walter Raleigh's bedroom was right beside a huge library he had, and Lockhart was puzzled, and he said, "What book? Which book?" And Sir Walter Raleigh said, "Son, there is only one book. Bring me the book." And Lockhart knew what he meant.[6]

I want to say to us today that there is just one. Let us pray.

O Lord, we thank You for the inspiration of the scriptures and not only for Your inspiration but for Your preservation. Despite the many attacks that have been made upon it, the many destructions it has gone through, the many who have committed to wiping it out, it still lasts, and it is still the book. Help us to believe it, treasure it, read it, and apply it to our lives. In Jesus's name. Amen.

NOTES

1. David Gibson, Religion News Service, Jan. 22, 2001.
2. http://en.wikipedia.org
3. Aharon Ronald Ellis Agus, "The 'Ladder' of R. Phinehas be Yair," in *Hermeneutic Biography in Rabbinic Midrash: The Body of this Death and Life* (Berline: de Gruyter, 1996), 91-200.
4. Samuel A. Cartledge, *The Bible: God's Word to Man* (Nashville: Broadman Press, 1968), 74
5. W. A. Criswell, *The Bible for Today's World* (Nashville: Broadman Press, 1965), 117.
6. Ibid., 24-25.

THOUGHT PROVOKERS

I do not take Jesus's words literally when he said if your eye looks upon another lustfully, you should gouge it out and throw it away.

"You have heard that it was said, 'You shall not commit adultery. But I tell you that anyone who looks at a woman lustfully has already committed adultery with her in his heart. If your right eye causes you to stumble, gouge it out and throw it away. It is better for you to lose one part of your body than for your whole body to be thrown into hell. And if your right hand causes you to stumble, cut it off and throw it away. It is better for you to lose one part of your body than for your whole body to go into hell" (Matt. 5:27-30 NIV).

CHAPTER 4

I Do Not Take Literally the Bible as Inerrant or Infallible

SERMON SYLLABUS

Text: 1 Corinthians 7:6, 10, 17, 25, 40

CIT: Paul knew that he was writing his own personal opinion about some things.

Thesis: The first claim to be made of scripture is not its inerrancy or infallibility but its authority.

Purpose:
- Major Objective: Doctrinal
- Specific Objective: Through the power of the Holy Spirit, I hope to lead each of us in trusting the claims the scripture makes for itself.

Introduction

Outline:
  I.   The Bible Is Not the Origin of Inerrant or Infallible
  II. The Bible Is Not Inerrant or Infallible in Its Science—Joshua 10:12-15
  III. The Bible Is Not Inerrant or Infallible in Its History—Matthew 27:5; Acts 1:18-20
  IV. The Bible Is Not Inerrant or Infallible in Its Politics—Romans 13:1-7
  V.   The Bible Is Not Inerrant or Infallible in Its Humanity—Leviticus 25:44-46; Exodus 21:7-11; Ephesians 6:5; 1 Timothy 6:1-4

Conclusion

THE WORD OF THE LORD

If you will notice, all of these come from chapter 7 of 1 Corinthians, but they are just parts of sentences. I encourage you in your private time of reading and devotion to read this chapter in its entirety, but I hope you will see the point being made as we read these statements.

1 Corinthians 7:6
"I say this as a concession, not as a command."

1 Corinthians 7:10
"To the married I give this command."

1 Corinthians 7:17
"This is the rule I lay down in all the churches."

1 Corinthians 7:25
"Now about virgins: I have no command from the Lord, but I give a judgment as one who by the Lord's mercy is trustworthy."

1 Corinthians 7:40
"In my judgment, she is happier if she stays as she is—and I think that I too have the Spirit of God."

INTRODUCTION

The point is that on the five occasions you have just read Paul saying, "In my judgment, I don't have a word from the Lord about this subject, so here is my opinion, etc." There is no indication anywhere in all of Paul's Epistles that he believed that the words that he was writing to the churches were words that were going to be canonized as scripture. There is no indication that Paul had that understanding. So, Preacher, are you saying Paul was not inspired? Not at all. I personally believe Paul's writings were inspired of the Spirit of God, but I point out the fact of the human element in our scripture. Our Bible did not drop down on golden plates like the Book of Mormon. Our Bible, unlike the Koran, was not verbally whispered on a mountaintop into a person's ears by an angel of God. This book was written through inspiration to human beings who wrote what God impressed upon them to write, and in this situation, Paul said, "No, I don't have a word from the Lord, but I do have the Spirit of the Lord, and here is what I believe. In my judgment, this is what I say."

We believe, I believe, that we take the scriptures most seriously when we take them nonliterally, historically, and inspired.

I. The Bible Is Not the Origin of Inerrant or Infallible

I received an email from an elder in a Presbyterian church in McAllen, Texas, this week. Can you believe people know about us way out in Texas? Well, apparently he had gotten one of our bulletins from somewhere. It was a very sincere email, and he wanted me to know that he was praying for my soul and for you, my church. And it all came down to the point that we do not take the scriptures literally. And then he made the statement that our scriptures are infallible. Human beings are fallible; our scriptures are not.

Well, let's look at that. The Bible claims for itself inspiration. The Greek word (theopneustos) means "God breathed." God breathed upon these writers of old, and they wrote down as they were led. Did they maintain their personalities? Yes. Did they maintain their poor grammar? Yes. Peter for one. God did not blot out their personalities. God spoke through their personalities. The word *inerrant* means "without error." *Infallible* means, according to Webster, "incapable of error." So when people use the words *inerrant* and *infallible*, they are saying that this book is without error in any form and is beyond the capability of having an error in it.

These two words have not been a part of biblical theology. They came into usage in the early '70s and all through the '80s, and they did so because of the rise of humanism and the apparent threat to the authenticity of the scriptures. So theologians and schools, *Christianity Today*—a magazine that promoted this big battle over infallibility and inerrancy that was led by Carl Henry—and a book called *The Battles of the Bible* written by Harold Lindsell were the people who were right up front and created these two words as their biblical beliefs.

The Bible does not claim inerrancy for itself. The Bible does not claim infallibility for itself. The Bible claims to be inspired of God, and that is enough. It is for me. So I will write our friend in Texas and attempt to educate him and tell him that he needs to pray and we need his prayers. I will take that. But we take our scriptures seriously, and I believe one can take them more seriously when one does not take them literally, because those proponents of inerrancy and infallibility believe that the scriptures are inerrant and infallible in every field.

In science, history, politics, sociology, or the humanities, in any area you want to mention, they claim the Bible is inerrant and infallible, but here is one of the ways they get away from it: the original autographs are infallible. Well, that is a neat argument since we do not have any of the originals. We do not have one original manuscript. So yeah, I can argue that the original manuscripts were without error. If there is any error that creeps in, it creeps in through the translation. Well, you cannot disprove that because the original manuscripts do not exist. Or if they exist, we have not yet archeologically found them. So I want to point out a couple of those areas, and they are in your text for today.

II. THE BIBLE IS NOT INERRANT OR INFALLIBLE IN ITS SCIENCE—JOSHUA 10:12-15

The Bible is not inerrant and infallible when it comes to science. It is not a science textbook. It was never meant to be. You go to the book of Joshua, chapter 10, that classic passage you have heard me use time and time again where Joshua prays and the sun stands still according to the Bible. Well, that didn't happen. That cannot happen. The sun does not move. Every experience of humankind tells us when we stand here and look at that beautiful sunset right over there—and I watch it many nights during the week if I get home early enough—everything about our experience says that that sun is dropping, moving. My little granddaughter says, "Bye." Nothing about my experience tells me that what I am standing on is moving. Nothing. From experience, you cannot make me believe that the Earth I am standing on is turning and that sun is standing still. So that is how they wrote it down.

They wrote it down out of their experience and their understanding, but we know that the sun does not revolve around the Earth; the Earth revolves around the sun. We know that. Though there are a few of us who still don't believe that. And there are a few of us who still believe the

Earth is flat. The Bible presents the Earth as flat. I had a person say to me, "Where do you get that at?" I said, "Go read Revelation 7:1. You have four angels standing on the four corners of the Earth. If you have four corners of the Earth, you've got a flat earth. There is no other way you can interpret that."

The Earth is not flat. The sun does not revolve around the Earth. The Earth revolves around the sun. The Bible is in fact in error when it presents its science. But it presented it out of their understanding of what life was about and their understanding of how the world worked. They could do it no other way. So the Bible is in error when it talks about its science.

III. THE BIBLE IS NOT INERRANT OR INFALLIBLE IN ITS HISTORY—MATTHEW 27:5; ACTS 1:18-20

The Bible is in error in its history. I will only use one point. I could use a hundred. In chapter 27 of Matthew, it says that Judas, when Jesus was killed, felt such remorse that he took the thirty pieces of silver to the high priests, threw the thirty pieces of silver at their feet, and said he had sinned. Matthew chapter 27 says he went out and hanged himself. It also says that the chief priest picked up the money and said, "This is blood money. We cannot put it in the temple treasury." So they went out and bought a potter's field that became a graveyard for immigrants and folks with no money. Presumably that is where Jesus was buried. But if you go to Acts chapter 1, it says that Judas took the thirty pieces of silver and went and bought the property himself, and while he was on the property, he fell headlong onto the ground. He hit with such force that he had internal bleeding and exposure to the point of death.

Now, you really have to push those two stories to make them harmonize. But the point is that there are hundreds of stories just like that. Well, how did it happen? As these stories emerge, as stories will, here is one version and here is another version. One writer writes down this version, and one writer writes down that version. To me that is the greater authenticity of the scriptures than if everyone agreed about everything.

If you parade four people into court, and four people get up on the witness stand and tell the same identical story using the same kinds of words, what is the judge going to do? Throw them out and maybe even put them in jail for perjury. All of our stories do not jive. So it makes sense that when the gospel writers tell one story this way and a different writer tells it that way that is evidence to me of the authenticity of it. But if you are going to hold to inerrancy and infallibility, you can't make it work. So the Bible is in error when it comes to its science, and it is in error when it comes to its history. Neither is it inerrant when it comes to its politics.

IV. THE BIBLE IS NOT INERRANT OR INFALLIBLE IN ITS POLITICS—ROMANS 13:1-7

Let me read you Romans 13:1-7, and I encourage you to read the whole thing at home. "Everyone must submit himself to the governing authorities, for there is no authority except that which God has established. The authorities that exist have been established by God. Consequently, he who rebels against the authority is rebelling against what God has instituted, and those who do so will bring judgment on themselves." (Rom, 13:1-2)

Now what has that just said? That has just said that when we dethroned Saddam Hussein, we brought God's judgment home. Because the only way that Saddam Hussein was in authority was because God put him there. You with me? The only power Hitler had was the power and authority that God gave him, and we did the world a great injustice against God's will when we took out Hitler. Godless communist leaders were established by God. I don't think so.

I do not take this text literally. I take it in the context of its history. And in the context of its history, here is what Paul faced: he faced a radical bunch of dagger-carrying Jews who were constantly getting into trouble with the Roman government, which was the oppressor and occupier, and there were zealous Jews who continued to fight to try to overthrow the Romans, and Paul was trying to bring control in the midst of chaos so Christianity could at least catch on and have enough life to begin to grow without being destroyed by the Roman government. So Paul said to them, "These powers and authorities were placed here by God. Stop all this uprising."

So if we are going to take that and make it literal, we better never march against another government. We had better not pull down another statue in the name of democracy and freedom, because we are going against the will and authority of God. Are you with me? Does that not make sense?

If one takes this passage as it is interpreted, and you must interpret it in the context of its original history. Take it out of the context of its original history, and you make monkeys fly.

Just like with its politics, the Bible is not inerrant and infallible in its humanity.

V. The Bible Is Not Inerrant or Infallible in Its Humanity—Leviticus 25:44-46; Exodus 21:7-11; Ephesians 6:5; 1 Timothy 6:1-4

Leviticus chapter 25 not only says that Israel could own slaves and that slaves became property of the master, but it also said that when a slave bore children, the children became property of the master. That passage goes on to say that if an Israelite father got into financial trouble, he could sell his daughter into slavery. Sorry, women, he could not sell the son. But as you know, women were property anyway in that day and time. We cannot accept that standard of humanity today. It must be rejected. We cannot own other human beings. Did Jesus have one word to say about opposition to slavery? No, He did not. I have wished a thousand times that He had, but He did not. Slavery was a product of His day.

Deuteronomy chapter 21 says that if you have a rebellious child, a willful, strong-willed child that will not be obedient, you spank him. No. It says you stone him to death. Go home and read it. If we carried that out literally today, how many children would we have? I would be batting zero out of four. There were times I wanted to do the Bill Crosby thing: "I brought you into this world; I will take you out." But you can't do that. But if you read the scriptures, it is there.

Within Leviticus chapter 20 is all the stuff we have batted around for so long now about homosexuality. At a Presbyterian meeting, when they said, "We have to take the Bible literally," I then said, "Why don't we?" Leviticus chapter 20 says kill all the homosexuals. Let's don't even talk about ordaining them. Let's just kill them. Let's just line them all up and kill them. You want to be obedient to the Bible? That is what the Bible says: just line them up and kill them. We can do it quicker today. We don't have to use stones. We've got machine guns. Let's just line them up.

We stand around talking about how we take the Bible literally; no we do not. We need to quit fostering that lie because it is turning thousands of people away. "I will not be a part of that group called Christians," they say. "They are just absolutely ignorant." Thousands of people are turned away over this one issue. We do not take the Bible literally. We need to quit using the word. We take it interpretively. In the thesis statement of this sermon, I said that the Bible's main proclamation is not inerrancy or infallibility; it is authority, and the Bible is the authority on salvation. The Bible is the authority on grace.

CONCLUSION

C.S. Lewis was attending a theological conference in England and the topic was "Is There Anything that Is Absolutely Unique to Christianity?" And C.S. Lewis said, "Absolutely and it is grace." And it is. Follow the eight paths of Buddhism, follow the law of Israel, follow the commands of Islam; none of them offer what Christianity offers, and that is a clear path of grace to God.[1]

Tony Capello[2] was in Honolulu. He went down for a revival, got there at a weird time, got up, and wanted something to eat. It was 3:00 in the morning, so he went down the street to this café and had a meal. At 3:30, a group of prostitutes came in, and they were loud, obnoxious, and vulgar. He started to leave, but something arrested his attention; a prostitute by the name of Agnes said to her girlfriends that tomorrow was her birthday. And one of the girlfriends snapped, "Well, you want me to get you a cake or something?" They laughed it down, and then they finally left.

Tony went to the restaurant owner and said, "Do they come in here regularly?" And the owner said, "Yes, you can set your watch by it; at 3:30 every morning they are in here. Just got off work, I guess." And Tony said, "Did you hear that girl that said it was her birthday?" He said, "Yes." "Who was that?" Tony asked. "Her name is Agnes," the owner said. And Tony said, "I would like to pay for a big birthday party in the morning at 3:30." And the owner laughed and said, "That is great. I will get the cake. You pay for it. I will get it."

So the next morning at about 1:30, Tony went to the restaurant and hung up balloons and all kinds of party stuff throughout the diner. They came in with the cake, and they waited, and at exactly 3:30, the group of prostitutes who knew each other came in. As they came in, Tony led the crowd in singing "Happy Birthday" to Agnes. She broke down into tears, picked up her cake, and said, "Can I run this two blocks down the street and show it to my mama? I have never ever had a birthday party or a cake." Agnes came back with that cake, singing "Happy Birthday" to Agnes. And Tony gathered that group of prostitutes in prayer and thanked God for them and thanked God for Agnes and asked God's grace to be upon them. That, my friends, is the authority of scripture. It is the grace that God in Christ Jesus offers to us. Let us pray.

Lord Jesus, we thank You for this word that was inspired by Your Spirit, preserved for Your Spirit, and is alive, infused by Your Spirit today. May we be willing and open for Your Spirit to touch us, move us, and change us even today. In Jesus's name. Amen.

Notes

1. Philip Yancey. *What's so Amazing about Grace?* (Grand Rapids: Zondervan Publishing House, 1997), 45.
2. Martin Thielen, *What's the Least I can Believe and Still be a Christian?* (Louisville: Westminster Press, 2011), 84-85.

THOUGHT PROVOKERS

I do not take literally the Bible's worldview that the Earth is flat with four corners.

"After this I saw four angels standing at the four corners of the earth, holding back the four winds of the earth to prevent any wind from blowing on the land or on the sea or on any tree" (Rev. 7:1 NIV).

Or that hell is below: "In hell, where he was in torment, he looked up and saw Abraham far away, with Lazarus by his side" (Luke 16:23 NIV).

Or that heaven is up: "After he said this, he was taken up before their very eyes, and a cloud hid him from their sight. They were looking intently up into the sky as he was going, when suddenly two men dressed in white stood beside them. 'Men of Galilee,' they said, 'why do you stand here looking into the sky? This same Jesus, who has been taken from you into heaven, will come back the same way you have seen him go into the sky'" (Acts 1:9-11 NIV).

CHAPTER 5

I Take Seriously the Bible's Account of God's Creation of Everything

Sermon Syllabus

Text: Genesis 1:1; Psalm 19:1-2; John 1:1-5

CIT: God created heaven and earth, establishing a perfect order.

Thesis: The planetary system God created is absolutely perfect.

Purpose:
- Major Objective: Doctrinal
- Specific Objective: Through the power of the Holy Spirit, I hope to lead each of us into a deeper relationship of awe related to God's creation.

Introduction

Outline:
I.   The Earth Is Tilting Perfectly
II. The Earth Is Rotating Perfectly
III. The Earth Is Wobbling Upward Perfectly
IV. The Earth Is Wobbling Downward Perfectly
V.   The Earth's Oceans Are Proportionately Perfect
VI. The Earth's Surface Is Proportionately Perfect
VII. The Earth Orbits the Sun Perfectly
VIII. The Earth's Distance from the Sun Is Perfect
IX. The Earth's Distance from the Moon Is Perfect
X.   The Earth's Oxygen Is Proportionately Perfect

Conclusion

INTRODUCTION

I believe with every fiber of my being that God created this marvelous universe, this wonderful Mother Earth that we exist upon, but I am more than a little out of my discipline this morning. My specialty is psychology and theology; it is not science. But I am dabbling in scientific information this morning. And for those of you who claim science as your discipline, I ask for your understanding and probably forgiveness of my oversimplification of your discipline.

So please keep that in mind as we walk through this sermon this morning, but the essence of what I want to say is that we live on a marvelously designed planet that is in the context of a beautifully designed galaxy among millions and millions of other galaxies, and I do not believe it happened by chance. I am going to ask for a couple of helpers this morning. Chance Kahler, if you would come and take this chair right here. Chance is going to help me illustrate the sermon this morning.

I have in this Crown Royal bag (and one of you left this bag at my house) ten quarters, and they are marked with a magic marker with numbers one through 10. I have ten points of my sermon this morning. Don't get excited; they are going to be really brief points, so we are not going to be here until noon. At each point, Chance is going to pull out one of these quarters and look at the number. If he lays out these quarters in sequence from one to ten, he is going to get these ten quarters, plus I am going to give him ten crisp $100 dollar bills. So he has a chance this morning of making $1,000. If there are mathematicians among us, you might tell him later what kind of chances he had.

But since it is my personal money, I want to safeguard it a little bit, so I am going to ask my granddaughter Sheldon if she would come and sit beside Chance to keep an eye on him. Not that I don't trust him or anything, but what Chance is going to do is reach into that bag, pull out a quarter, and show her the number, and she is going to write the number down on one of those ten pieces of paper. He is going to put the quarter back in the bag, shake it up, pull out a second quarter, and show it to her, and she will write the number down. He will then put it back in the bag and shake it up, etc. We will go through that process ten times. Good luck to you, my friend.

And those of you mathematicians who are working on what kind of odds Chance has . . . I started to say 'someone,' but I will just go ahead and confess it was his daddy, Dr. Kahler, who said, "Well, if he lays them all out one through ten, we probably need to burn him at the stake." And I said, "Yeah, the pastor along with him too." All right, after I read our text, I will nod to you, Chance, and you can pull out the first quarter.[1]

Our text today is three sections of scripture, first from Genesis, that beautiful poem of creation, and then from Psalm 19:1-2 and John 1:1-5.

THE WORD OF THE LORD

Genesis 1:1
"In the beginning God created the heavens and the earth."

Psalm 19:1-2
"The heavens declare the glory of God; the skies proclaim the work of his hands. Day after day they pour forth speech; night after night they reveal knowledge."

John 1:1-5
"In the beginning was the Word, and the Word was with God, and the Word was God. He was with God in the beginning. Through him all things were made; without him nothing was made that has been made. In him was life, and that life was the light of all mankind. The light shines in the darkness, and the darkness has not overcome it."

I. THE EARTH IS TILTING PERFECTLY

Chance, you can pull out quarter number one. The Earth is not perpendicularly upright. The Earth is tilting 23 degrees. That 23 degrees is absolutely perfect. If it were upright in its rotation, life as we know it would not exist, and that will get clearer in just a minute. So the first quarter, could the Earth have lined itself up in a perfect 23 degree angle as it rotates around the sun by chance? That is the first quarter.

II. The Earth Is Rotating Perfectly

Chance, you can take out the second one. As the Earth exists at this 23 degree angle, it is rotating perfectly on its axis. Our Mother Earth turns at 1,000 miles per hour. She is spinning 1,000 miles per hour. Have you ever traveled at 1,000 miles per hour? Well, you can tell your friends you have because you are right now. The Earth on her axis spins 1,000 miles per hour.

That speed is perfect to what our life needs. If Mother Earth slowed down to 100 miles per hour instead of 1,000, our days would be ten times as long or five times as long. Think about that. A day like today times five means no cooling in the evening, no night skies. You would have this kind of heat for five days straight, five twenty-four-hour days. If that were true, our plant life could not exist. It would burn out and scorch in the July and August heat. But think about January and February. If we had a winter like we had this past winter, you would have five days of night, twenty-four hours times five of no sunshine. The temperatures would drop so low that life as we know it could not exist. So not only is Mother Earth tilted at a 23 degree angle, just perfect for life as we know it, but she is spinning on her axis at 1,000 miles per hour, which is just perfect to create the kind of temperature we live in day by day.

III. The Earth Is Wobbling Upward Perfectly

Take out the third quarter, Chance. As Mother Earth rotates on this 23 degree angle, she wobbles upward 3 degrees. In her wobbling upward three degrees (and you can take out the next quarter, Chance) she also wobbles downward three degrees. Keep in mind now our beautiful Earth is at a 23 degree angle and is traveling on her axis at 1,000 miles per hour. She also wobbles upward 3 degrees. Not 4, not 6, and not sometimes 3 and sometimes 2, but she wobbles upward 3 degrees perfectly every time.

IV. The Earth Is Wobbling Downward Perfectly

She also wobbles down 3 degrees perfectly every time. And this wobbling upward and downward 3 degrees each time creates for us our four seasons.

Were it not for this wobbling upward and downward, we would not have the seasons we have. If she wobbled 6 degrees, life as we know it could not exist. If she wobbled downward 6 degrees, life as we know it could not exist. She has to wobble upward perfectly 3 degrees every time, and she has to wobble downward perfectly 3 degrees every time. Is there a chance that this developed randomly? I don't think so!

V. THE EARTH'S OCEANS ARE PROPORTIONATELY PERFECT

Pull out quarter number five, Chance. I read that the oceans are perfect in their depth. If there were ten more feet of ocean depth, that would be so much added moisture in our atmosphere that we could not make it.

VI. THE EARTH'S SURFACE IS PROPORTIONATELY PERFECT

Pull out another quarter, Chance. Our Earth's crust is perfect in its depth. If it were ten feet deeper, we would have so much material life using the oxygen there, we could not make it. So our ocean's depth and the crust of our Mother Earth are perfect in proportion. If either one of them was out of proportion, we could not live and exist as we do.

VII. THE EARTH ORBITS THE SUN PERFECTLY

Quarter number seven, Chance. The Earth orbits our sun at 18 miles per second. Eighteen miles per second in her orbit around the sun. I have gone over this many, many times with you. It is our experience that our sun is moving, and that is the way we talk about it. The sun goes down, and the sun comes up, but as we know, the sun does not move. Our sun stands still. It is Mother Earth that does the rotating. And as she is spinning 1,000 miles per hour on her axis, she is orbiting the sun at 18 miles per second. Now, if you change that to 12 miles per second, that would slow us down, we would be drawn closer to the sun, and we would scorch. So she is traveling 18 miles per second, which is perfect to keep us in the temperatures we have today. So everything to this point is absolutely perfect, and it has to be that way for us to exist.

VIII. The Earth's Distance from the Sun Is Perfect

Draw out the next quarter, Chance. We are 93 million miles from the sun. The distance from Mother Earth to the sun is 93 million miles. The sun's surface is 11,000 to 12,000 degrees in temperature. Asbestos melts at 4,000 degrees. Could we exist closer than we are? Not at all. Could we exist farther away than we are? Not at all. We would freeze in the winters. Any closer, and we would scorch in the summers. Our Mother Earth is rotating that magnificent sun that is 93 million miles away in perfect order. Are you beginning to get the picture? How are we doing on the quarters, Chance?

IX. The Earth's Distance from the Moon Is Perfect

Pull out another one, Chance. We are 240,000 miles from the moon. We have been there. Right? I know folks who still don't believe we have been there. They say it was some movie they put on TV. We haven't been to the moon. The government is tricking us. Well, I believe we have been to the moon. I believe there is clear evidence of that. I think we have some rocks we brought back, don't we? But I guess we could have gotten them from the Mohave Desert.

At 240,000 miles away the moon is perfect. Her pull, her gravitational pull on us, is absolutely perfect in bringing in the tide and taking it out. I remember years ago—I was about eighteen, I believe—I was at a fishing store, buying some bait at Myrtle Beach, and there was a tidal chart that told me exactly what time the tide would come in and what time it would go out for a full year in advance. I remember looking at that and saying, "Wow! How can that be? How can we predict a year from now at what time the morning that tide will come in and what time she will go out?" That is really not a prediction because that tidal chart, if done right, will be absolutely perfect. And you know why? Because Mother Moon is going to bring it in with that gravitational pull absolutely perfectly every time.

There are places in our world where the tidal difference between low tide and high tide is 63 feet. We have seen some tsunami tides created by underocean earthquakes. But what if we were half that distance from Mother Moon? What would her gravitational pull do to us? Can you imagine what half the distance would do when she reached down and pulled up the Atlantic Ocean and brought it across flat Texas and Mexico and crashed it into the Rocky Mountains? Can you imagine what would be created? A hurricane going in and a hurricane going back out. But at 240,000 miles away, her gravitational pull is absolutely perfect. Did that happen by chance? I don't think so. How are we doing on the quarters, Chance?

X. The Earth's Oxygen Is Proportionately Perfect

Pull out the last one, Chance. Our oxygen is absolutely perfect for what we need for life on Mother Earth. And here is where I just dabble a little bit, and I know a little about a lot of stuff. You know people like that? They know a little bit about a lot of things, but they don't know a whole lot about anything. But I believe—and forgive me dear botany people because I am really going to oversimplify here—that every little blade of grass and every plant life and every leaf on these trees takes in moisture from Mother Earth's bowels and sunshine from Father Sun and creates within it cells. And these plant cells produce a starch, and our entire planet depends upon this starch because we need it. It sustains us. Our animals eat it, and it sustains them, and we eat them. Without photosynthesis, we could not exist. If these plants did not create plant cells that create starch that sustains us, we could not live. Not only that, but they balance the oxygen in our atmosphere. If we didn't starve to death, we would asphyxiate.

Conclusion

I could go on and on, but here are ten things that have to operate absolutely perfectly for us to exist. By chance, here is how the quarters laid out: 1, 7, 7, 7, 4, 8, 8, 3, 8, 8. All right mathematicians, tell me what kind of chance Mr. Kahler had. They tell me one in 3 billion. So I was safe with Mama's thousand dollars in my pocket today. Thank you, Chance. Thank you, Sheldon.

I realize the psalmist of Psalm 19 did not know all of this when he stood with this deep sense of awe and reverence and said to God, "Your handiwork speaks all day, and the magnificence of the stars speak of your glory all night." What a marvelous design coming from a magnificent designer our world is. To me it cannot be a random act. It cannot be a coming together. Our planetary system was designed and created by a master, the master craftsman, and we enjoy the bliss of her today. As we celebrate this day of freedom, let us also celebrate this magnificent creation we live in, and let us celebrate it with gratitude every day when we get up in the morning. For God's marvelous perfect universe has given us another day to just thoroughly enjoy. Let us pray.

O Lord, thank You for Mother Earth, this galaxy, and all the other galaxies we do not even know exist yet. For Your magnificent creation that is so perfectly designed and gives us life and sustenance day after day, to You be praise. Help us each and every day to lift our thoughts and lift our words of praise, awe, reverence, and adoration to You for Your marvelous love of us in creating, designing, and implementing such a marvelous Mother Earth. To You be praise, and to You be glory. In Jesus's name. Amen.

NOTES

1. I was impressed to use the ten coins by a sermon I heard at Southwestern Baptist Theological Seminary by Professor Tolar in 1976.

THOUGHT PROVOKERS

I do not literally believe that all of humankind descended from the first couple, Adam and Eve. *Adam* is a transliteration of the Hebrew word *Adom*, which in the Hebrew means "men."

"Then the LORD God formed a man from the dust of the ground and breathed into his nostrils the breath of life, and the man became a living being" (Gen. 2:7 NIV).

> The Lord God said, "It is not good for the man to be alone. I will make a helper suitable for him."
>
> Now the Lord God had formed out of the ground all the wild animals and all the birds in the sky. He brought them to the man to see what he would name them; and whatever the man called each living creature, that was its name. So the man gave names to all the livestock, the birds in the sky and all the wild animals.
>
> But for Adam no suitable helper was found. So the Lord God caused the man to fall into a deep sleep; and while he was sleeping, he took one of the man's ribs and then closed up the place with flesh. Then the Lord God made a woman from the rib he had taken out of the man, and he brought her to the man.
>
> The man said, "This is now bone of my bones and flesh of my flesh; she shall be called 'woman,' for she was taken out of man."
>
> That is why a man leaves his father and mother and is united to his wife, and they become one flesh.
>
> Adam and his wife were both naked, and they felt no shame. (Gen. 2:18-25 NIV)

CHAPTER 6

I Do Not Take Literally Genesis's Account of Creation

Sermon Syllabus

Text: Genesis 1:1-2:4

CIT: Genesis was a beautiful poem of creation telling that God created everything.

Thesis: Genesis is a poem of creation, and we do not take the words of a poem literally.

Purpose:
- Major Objective: Doctrinal
- Specific Objective: Through the power of the Holy Spirit, I hope to lead each of us in affirming the reality of God's creation.

Introduction

Outline:
I. Genesis's Creation Story Was Written as a Poem
II. Genesis's Creation Poem Is Not in Logical Sequence—Genesis 1:3, 14
III. Genesis's First Creation Poem Is in Conflict With the Second Creation Poem—Genesis1:26-27; 2:7, 18-25
IV. Genesis's Creation Poem Is Not Really Concerned with Six Days—Psalms 90:4

Conclusion

INTRODUCTION

Of those of you who were here last Sunday, how many of you believe that I believe that our planetary system was created by God? Is there anybody here this week who was here last week who does not believe that? I see no hands. Good. I am glad I have established that. There is no question in my mind that the marvelous Mother Earth that we enjoy and the planetary system that does all this integral details to support her just did not happen.

It is the old philosophical theory of where there is a watch, there is a watchmaker. If you are walking in the woods and come up on a pocket watch, and you look at it, and you do not think, *Ah, look at all these wheels and cogs. Somebody just threw them or the wind kept blowing them and blowing them until they just came together working to give me a precise time of day.* No, you look at it and think, *Wow! There must be a watchmaker.* So we look at the marvelous details of our planetary system, and I don't know how we can come to any other conclusion other than that there is a grand design and a grand designer of our planetary system.

Now that everybody understands that and where I am coming from, let's look at our creation story that tells us that God created everything. If you will notice in your bulletin, it is a long text, but I could not divide it up. It is the creation story. I had Toni print it in the New English version because it illustrates a little more clearly that I think it is poetry. I will be reading from the New International Standard that we always read from, which will be a little different from yours, but think with me as we read it together, you reading silently. Let's think together about the poetic structure of this beautiful piece of material, and it is, in my estimation, a masterpiece.

THE WORD OF THE LORD

Genesis 1:1-2:4

> In the beginning God created the heavens and the earth. Now the earth was formless and empty, darkness was over the surface of the deep, and the Spirit of God was hovering over the waters.

And God said, "Let there be light," and there was light. God saw that the light was good, and he separated the light from the darkness. God called the light "day," and the darkness he called "night." And there was evening, and there was morning—the first day.

And God said, "Let there be a vault between the waters to separate water from water." So God made the vault and separated the water under the vault from the water above it. And it was so. God called the vault "sky." And there was evening, and there was morning—the second day.

And God said, "Let the water under the sky be gathered to one place, and let dry ground appear." And it was so. God called the dry ground "land," and the gathered waters he called "seas." And God saw that it was good.

Then God said, "Let the land produce vegetation: seed-bearing plants and trees on the land that bear fruit with seed in it, according to their various kinds." And it was so. The land produced vegetation: plants bearing seed according to their kinds and trees bearing fruit with seed in it according to their kinds. And God saw that it was good. And there was evening, and there was morning—the third day.

And God said, "Let there be lights in the vault of the sky to separate the day from the night, and let them serve as signs to mark sacred times, and days and years, and let them be lights in the vault of the sky to give light on the earth." And it was so. God made two great lights—the greater light to govern the day and the lesser light to govern the night. He also made the stars. God set them in the vault of the sky to give light on the earth, to govern the day and the night, and to separate light from darkness. And God saw that it was good. And there was evening, and there was morning—the fourth day.

And God said, "Let the water teem with living creatures, and let birds fly above the earth across the vault of the sky." So God created the great creatures of the sea and every living thing with which the water teems and that moves about in it, according to their kinds, and every winged bird according to its kind. And God saw that it was good. God blessed them and said, "Be fruitful and increase in number and fill the water in the seas, and let the birds increase on the earth." And there was evening, and there was morning—the fifth day.

And God said, "Let the land produce living creatures according to their kinds: the livestock, the creatures that move along the ground, and the wild animals, each according to its kind." And it was so. God made the wild animals according to their kinds, the livestock according to their kinds, and all the creatures that move along the ground according to their kinds. And God saw that it was good.

Then God said, "Let us make mankind in our image, in our likeness, so that they may rule over the fish in the sea and the birds in the sky, over the livestock and all the wild animals, and over all the creatures that move along the ground."

So God created mankind in his own image, in the image of God he created them; male and female he created them.

God blessed them and said to them, "Be fruitful and increase in number; fill the earth and subdue it. Rule over the fish in the sea and the birds in the sky and over every living creature that moves on the ground."

Then God said, "I give you every seed-bearing plant on the face of the whole earth and every tree that has fruit with seed in it. They will be yours for food. And to all the beasts of the earth and all the birds in the sky and all the creatures that move along the ground—everything that has the breath of life in it—I give every green plant for food." And it was so.

God saw all that he had made, and it was very good. And there was evening, and there was morning—the sixth day.

Thus the heavens and the earth were completed in all their vast array.

By the seventh day God had finished the work he had been doing; so on the seventh day he rested from all his work. Then God blessed the seventh day and made it holy, because on it he rested from all the work of creating that he had done.

I. Genesis's Creation Story Was Written as a Poem

We do not take poetry literally. When you come to this passage in the Hebrew language, it is very, very clear by the way it is written that one is reading poetry. By the fashion in which it is written, you know from the very reading that it is poetry. If you read poetry in English, no one has to tell you that what you are reading is poetry. You know by the design and the meter and the rhythm and all of that that it is poetry. The very fact that the way in which it is written gives you that information.

And when reading poetry, you do not take it literally. That beautiful poem titled "Immortality"[1] has two caterpillars talking to each other about their impending death. It is a beautiful poem, a classic, but caterpillars don't talk. Caterpillars do not worry about immortality. Caterpillars are just caterpillars. And what about that beautiful poem I had to memorize in high school, and maybe some of you did too, called "Said the Rose."[2] In it this rose speaks of how she is cut from the garden and carried to her mistress's room, and she is looking forward to this beautiful eternity, and lo and behold she starts dying, and her mistress throws her out into the garden. Roses do not talk. They do not worry about where they are going to end up. In another poem that I learned as a child, "Between the Owl and the Fox,"[3] the owl and the fox carry on a lengthy conversation. But owls and foxes do not talk. We do not take that literally.

And then there is Leo, the cat who talks to his mistress but only after he dies.[4] Leo the cat talks to his mistress to try to help her process her grief. Now come on. A talking cat? A talking dead cat? Come on. We do not take poetry literally. But poetry can carry us to the height of awe, respect, wonder, and clarity. What would our world be without the sublime words of poetry that have enriched our lives for centuries? This is a piece of poetry. We do not take it literally. Let me rephrase that. I do not take it literally. You can take it any way you want to take it. I know in reading the Hebrew that it is poetry, and I receive it as poetry, but it is a masterpiece.

Yesterday I was not well at all, so I spent the day in the house. Some kind of bug. So I researched once again the world's creation stories. I must have read a hundred. Every culture that has a written record, and some that do not have written records but have finally got them transmitted orally, has a creation story. Every culture. The Cherokee have several. I will just quickly tell you the ending of one. This great super buzzard comes down, and he flaps his wings everywhere. And as his wings go down, there is a valley, and as he brings them up, there is a mountain. And so this buzzard flies over Cherokee, North Carolina, with each flap of his wings creating these magnificently beautiful mountains that we look at. We don't take that literally. They are trying to share in poetry and myth and story what they believe about creation. You ask a Cherokee, and if he is sober he will tell you that is not a literal story. If he is drunk, he will tell you he saw it when it happened.

Every culture has a creation story, and our culture is no different. The Jewish culture is no different. This is a beautiful creation story. In fact, I challenge anyone to bring to me a more magnificently written creation story than this one. It flows. It is just magnificently superb.

Israel's neighbor Babylon had a creation story where Marduk, the male god, and the female goddess get in a fight, and Marduk overcomes her and cuts her body up, and her body becomes Mother Earth, and other parts of her become the other parts of the planetary system. Now, I re-read that yesterday, and I thought it was kind of gruesome, unlike this beautiful story we have before us today. Absolutely magnificent. So what it caused at least me to do is to realize that here are people of faith—the writers—who like everyone else in their day are trying to present to the world their belief in their god who created their world and their universe. When you take it as poetry you can truly see the simplicity and the beauty and the truth of what it is trying to portray, and that truth is that we have a created order, and that created order was by design by our creator.

Then this piece becomes unproblematic. You do not have a problem with evolution if you do not take Genesis literally. If you understand Genesis as a poem, you do not have a problem with evolution or other forms of science whatsoever. It is a poem. And being a poem, it is not logical in its sequence. Most poetry is not, and neither is this.

II. GENESIS'S CREATION POEM IS NOT IN LOGICAL SEQUENCE—GENESIS 1:3, 14

Let me just point out one example. In verse 3, it reads, "And God said." Did you notice that over and over, nine times it says, "And God said"? Nine times. Did you notice again that six times it reads, "And there was evening, and there was morning—the first day"; "And there was evening, and there was morning—the second day;" and so on? See the beauty of that? Verse 3 says, "And God said, 'Let there be light,' and there was light. God saw that the light was good, and he separated the light from the darkness. God called the light 'day,' and the darkness he called 'night.'"

Now verses 14 and 15: "And God said, 'Let there be light in the expanse of the sky to separate the day from the night. And let them serve as signs to mark seasons and days and years, and let them be lights in the expanse of the sky to give light on earth,' and it was so." God made two great lights, the greater light to govern the day, the lesser light to govern the night. He also made the stars. Isn't that just beautiful? Where did the first light come from? Where did the light come from in verse 3? The only light we have is from the sun, the moon, and the planetary system—the stars. That is where we get our light. Well, in verse 3, God created light and separated light from the darkness, from the night and the night from the day. And now He comes back and creates a sun, moon, and stars. But poetry is like that. So don't force this to be literal, because if you do, this is one of the problems it gets you into. It is not logical; it is not sequential. Poetry's intent is not to be logical or sequential.

III. GENESIS'S FIRST CREATION POEM IS IN CONFLICT WITH THE SECOND CREATION POEM—GENESIS 1:26-27; 2:7, 18-25

If you take it logically and literally, then you "have a problem" with the second creation story. The first creation story was written by the priestly writer. The second creation story was written by what we call the "J writer" or the Jehovah writer. These two stories were written by two different people at two different times. We know from research that the first creation story that I read came to Israel in about 586 BC while they were in captivity in Babylon. They already had the Adam and Eve story, but they created this beautiful story in poetry to demonstrate to the world that they were exiled in the majesty and the beauty of their God. You cannot make these two creation stories jive. I have read commentary after commentary that try. They just will not fit.

In the creation story, it says beautifully, "And God said, 'Let us make humankind in our image, and they created humankind. Male and female created he them." (Gen. 1:27)Well, that is a creation story. And then the other story gets into Adam and Eve. Creating Adam and creating Eve out of his side. You cannot make these stories reconcile with each other. They are not complimentary to each other. They were not intended to be. They are two entirely different stories. Both are beautiful poetry.[5]

Another problem you have is in verse 29 of our creation story. Verse 29 says, "Then God said, 'I give you every seed bearing plant on the face of the whole earth and every tree that has fruit with seed in it. They will be yours for food.'" So in this first creation story, God says to his creation you can eat anything, and everything has been given to you for food. (Gen, 1:29) But you know the second story. God creates Adam and Eve, and He says, "You can eat all this, except there is one you cannot eat thereof. It is the tree of knowledge. You cannot eat of it. If you do, you will die." (Gen.2:16-17) So again we have conflict. If you take it literally, we have conflicting issues between this first creation story and second creation story. But when you understand it as poetry, God is saying to us that this universe did not just happen, this planetary system did not just come together in this beautiful detailed way that works by itself. It has a creator, and God is saying, "I am that creator." Marvelous, marvelous story.

IV. GENESIS'S CREATION POEM IS NOT REALLY CONCERNED WITH SIX DAYS—PSALMS 90:4

And here is where I believe we make a big point over nothing. Do not take the six days literally. Psalm 90, and 1 Peter 3:8 say that with the Lord a day is as a thousand years, and a thousand years as a day. God is not bound by space and time. We are. We cannot think outside space and time. God, our sovereign, is outside of time and space. He is not limited by time and space. And the writers say a day with the Lord is like a thousand years and a thousand years as a day. But when you come to this beautiful poem of creation and you try to make it a literal six-day creation, you have all kinds of problems in reconciling that with any reputable science of today. Carbon-14 dating is one of the most precise sciences we have, and we know that this planet is 14 to 19 billion years old, not 6,000 years old. And we know that this planet and the solar system had an evolution to it. Not a quick six-day creation.

CONCLUSION

But you can take the Bible seriously, I believe, more seriously when you take it for what it is. It is the Word of God, inspired by God to say to God's creation what life is and where it came from, not *how* but *where* they came from and where their creator is and the love of their creator. When you do not make this creation story literal, the problems just go away. Let us pray.

Lord, thank You for this beautiful story. A story of creation, a beautiful poem giving us all the information we need, all the information we can understand. Information that points us to You, our creator, for the beauty of our planet, for the substance of our Mother Earth. We give You thanks and praise. But most of all we thank You for not only revealing Yourself through the Word but revealing Yourself in Jesus the Christ, who came and lived among us as one of us to show us, to demonstrate to us Your awesome love of us. To You be praise, and to You be glory for Your creation and Your redemption. In Jesus's name, amen.

NOTES

1. Joseph Jefferson, *The Best Loved Poems of the American People*, ed. Hazel Jelleman" (Garden City, NY: Doubleday and Company, Inc., 1926), 85-86.
2. Ibid., 7-10.
3. Ibid., 240-244.
4. Ibid., 589-590
5. Julis Wellhausaen, *Die Composition des Hexateuchs und der Historisheen Bucher des Alten Testaments* (Berlin: G. Rimer, 1899), 373. (BS 1215. W4 1899).

Note: Refer to pages 1-20 of *The Masks We Wear* by Eugene C. Rollins for a full explanation of the two creation stories.

THOUGHT PROVOKERS

I do not take literally the fact of robbing from God if I do not give 10 percent of my income to the church.

"Will a mere mortal rob God? Yet you rob me.

"But you ask, 'How are we robbing you?'

"In tithes and offerings. You are under a curse—your whole nation—because you are robbing me. Bring the whole tithe into the storehouse, that there may be food in my house. Test me in this," says the Lord Almighty, "and see if I will not throw open the floodgates of heaven and pour out so much blessing that there will not be room enough to store it." (Mal. 3:8-10 NIV)

CHAPTER 7

I Take the Bible Seriously When It Claims that God Owns Everything

Sermon Syllabus

Text: Psalm 24:1-2; Psalm 50:7-15; Haggai 2:8

CIT: The Bible said that God created everything and also owns everything.

Thesis: I myself belong to God, and also everything I claim as mine belongs to God.

Purpose:
- Major Objective: Doctrinal
- Specific Objective: Through the power of the Holy Spirit, I hope to lead each of us in being good stewards of God's creation.

Introduction

Outline:
    I.   We Belong to God—Psalm 24:1b
    II. Our World and Everything in It Belongs to God—Psalm 24:1a
    III. Our Wealth Belongs to God—Haggai 2:8
    IV. Our God Wants Our Thanksgiving—Psalm 50:14-15

Conclusion

The Word of the Lord

Psalm 24:1-2
"The earth is the LORD's, and everything in it, the world, and all who live in it; for he founded it on the seas and established it on the waters."

Psalm 50:7-15

> Listen, my people, and I will speak; I will testify against you, Israel: I am God, your God. I bring no charges against you concerning your sacrifices or concerning your burnt offerings, which are ever before me. I have no need of a bull from your stall or of goats from your pens, for every animal of the forest is mine, and the cattle on a thousand hills. I know every bird in the mountains, and the insects in the fields are mine. If I were hungry I would not tell you, for the world is mine, and all that is in it. Do I eat the flesh of bulls or drink the blood of goats? "Sacrifice thank offerings to God, fulfill your vows to the Most High, and call on me in the day of trouble; I will deliver you, and you will honor me.

Haggai 2:8
"The silver is mine and the gold is mine, declares the LORD Almighty."

Introduction

When I was in college and taking an English literature course from old Dr. Howard, he loved the poem "Invictus," and probably one of the reasons I fell in love with it was the fact that he loved it and because he was an educational mentor of mine. But I came to realize that I loved it for another reason. Written by William Ernest Henley, it goes like this:

> Out of the night that covers me,
> Black as the Pit from pole to pole,
> I thank whatever gods may be
> For my unconquerable soul.

> In the fell clutch of circumstance
> I have not winced nor cried aloud.
> Under the bludgeonings of chance

My head is bloody, but unbowed.
Beyond this place of wrath and tears
Looms but the Horror of the shade,
And yet the menace of the years
Finds, and shall find, me unafraid.

It matters not how strait the gate,
How charged with punishments the scroll.
I am the master of my fate:
I am the captain of my soul.[1]

I think I fell in love with that poem because it is everything that I am not. There is an arrogant, self-willed, noncompliant part of me who wants to be everything that poem is. But I am not. I am not the captain of my own soul. I am owned. I am doubly owned. I am created, as are you, in the image of God, God's spirit child. And as you are, I am redeemed by Jesus the Christ. Paul says in Romans 14:8, "If we live, we live unto the Lord. If we die, we die unto the Lord. Whether we live or whether we die, we belong to the Lord." And then in 1 Corinthians 6:19, he says, "You are not your own; you were bought at a price." So although there is a part of me that longs to be the person Henley talks about, I am not that person. I am not my own.

I. WE BELONG TO GOD—PSALM 24:1B

The psalmist told us we belong to God. You belong to God. I belong to God. Well, what does that mean in practical terms? What that means is that any decision we face, ordinary or extraordinary, is not our own to make. We are to consult with that great "Ally" that owns us.

When I had my faith experience, I was in the food business. I had been in the food business since I was ten. I loved the food business, had no problems with it. And after I was redeemed, I wanted to stay in the food business. I did not want to become a preacher. I did not even like preachers. I still don't like them. I surely did not want to be one. But I am not my own, and God called me into the ministry, and when I got clear about that call, I went because I am owned. I am not the captain of my own soul. In Texas, when I was pastoring and finished a master's degree out there, I loved Texas and never wanted to leave. I absolutely fell in love with the West. I did not want to come back to South Carolina, but I did because I am not my own.

I am owned, and so are you. We were bought with a price. In fact, the only place I have ever gone and wanted to go to was Liberty Hill. I fell in love with Liberty Hill when I came in 1984. A little handful of people up there fell in love with me and I with them, and it was not long after that that they called me as their preacher and that I purchased two pieces of property out there in the cemetery, and they thought, *Oh my gosh, we are never going to get rid of him.* And they were right. It has been a wonderful twenty-seven years here with these wonderful people at this most beautiful place. I thank God constantly for the privilege of being here. And I thank Him that He hasn't said, "Well, you know, I want you down in Louisiana or somewhere else."

But we are not our own, and when we apply that practically and think about all the decisions we have to make and the choices that come up, we realize that we have an "Ally" that will help us, guide us, and lead us if we will only consult, prayerfully consult, engage, and communicate with Him. Then we can make those decisions knowing that we have sought counsel with God on this and that this is where God wants us to go, this is what God wants us to do, and then when we do that and it all falls apart—and it often does—we know.

That is like when God called me to a little church in Texas, and it was really three churches—here, here, and here—and all three of them never spoke to the other one. Now patch that up, Preacher. So sometimes even when you know you are doing what the Lord wants you to do, there is all kinds of trouble and issues you have to deal with. I take seriously what the Bible says about God's ownership of me, and I encourage you to as well because it will radically alter the way you do business with your life.

II. OUR WORLD AND EVERYTHING IN IT BELONGS TO GOD—PSALM 24:1A

And then the scripture tell us that our world and everything in it belong to God. Did you get that? We are stewards. The Greek word for *steward* is a compound word: *Oiron* is the first word, which means "house." *Omos* is the second word, which means "law." So when you put them together, you get *oironomos*, and we are stewards of the home. When you think about that in relationship to all that we have and all that we call "mine," it is not really ours; it is the Lord's, and we are stewards of it. We are managers of it. Now boy, if you think that won't change your life view and your perspective on the stuff you have, it radically will.

I remember one day several years ago I was walking around on that little piece of property just around the cove that we call ours and that I call mine. I was walking around saying, "Well, my grass does look good this year. My trees are wonderfully healthy. My azaleas look good." I was thinking *my, my, my,* and then it suddenly dawned on me that in just a few short years, shorter now than they were then, someone else was going to be walking around on this same piece of property saying, "My grass, my tree, my azalea bushes, my gardenia bushes."

Linda and I were talking about that the other night, and I said to her, "You know, when that happens, please don't let the new man have my new golf clubs." And she said "I won't. He is left-handed." Isn't it amazing how we just claim all this stuff, and when we really claim it—*it is mine*—we get really possessive and protective of it. When we can release it, we do it within our deepest awareness, knowing that this belongs to God, and we are managers of it.

III. Our Wealth Belongs to God—Haggai 2:8

And then that beautiful passage in Haggai says, "I own the silver, and I own the gold." Not only does God own us, not only does God own everything that is, but God owns our wealth. Well now, wait a minute, Preacher. I worked hard for it. It is mine. No, it is really not, and one day you will find out. You know, that is what Ecclesiastes was so upset about. The writer of Ecclesiastes was the first existentialist to ever write. Listen to it:

> So I hated life because it is work that is done under the sun was grievous to me. All of it meaningless a chasing after the wind. I hated all the things I had toiled for under the sun because I must leave them to the one who comes after me. And who knows whether he will be a wise man or a fool, yet he will have control over all the work into which I have poured my effort and skill

under the sun. This too is meaningless. So my heart began to despair over all my toils of labor under the sun for a man may do his work with wisdom, knowledge and skill and then he must leave it, all he owns to someone who has not worked for it. This a great meaninglessness. What does a man get for all his toil and anxious striving with which he labors under the sun. All his days work is pain and grief even at night his mind does not rest. This too is meaningless. (Eccles. 3:17-23)

Wow. That is what material things will leave you with. When you keep striving and working, thinking, *I've got to acquire this, I've got to acquire that, I've got to have this new toy, I got to have that new toy. Oh, if I could just put a little more in the bank, I will feel more secure. I just get a little more stock, a little more real estate, and I will feel better about myself and all that I have done.* No, no, a thousand times no. All our wealth belongs to God, the scripture says, and we are stewards of that.

I mentioned how happy I have been at Liberty Hill over these years. Here is one of the things that has made me happy: in twenty-seven years, we have not done one stewardship program. Not one. The first year I was here, I outlined the stewardship program. We were going to have pledge cards like all other stewardship programs, and the church mother, Margaret Richards, came to me and said, "Gene, I don't want you to do that." And I said, "Well, we have to have money coming in, Margaret. I've got to get paid. And you know there are other things we've got to pay like the light bill." And she said, "Trust us." I said, "Beg your pardon?" She said, "Tell us what you need and trust us." I said, "I tell you what I will do, Margaret. I won't do a stewardship campaign this year. And every year that you meet your budget, I will not do a stewardship campaign. But the year you miss your budget, we will have a stewardship campaign." And she said, "Fair enough."

Twenty-seven years later, we have not had a stewardship campaign. Per capita, Liberty Hill is the highest giver in our synod. South Carolina, Georgia, Florida—that is our synod. Little old Liberty Hill. I didn't tell you that until just a few years ago. I didn't want you to get a big head and quit giving. But what we have done all these years is—I tell you, people—what we need and what we have got to have, and you just come through with it. And really, that is the way it ought to be.

I have people almost every week who call and say, "Preacher, I want to talk to you about this fund-raising campaign. We got peanuts to sell." I say, "No. We don't do that stuff here." Now, we have done things like that for the Manse Committee Fund, but we don't do pledge cards for the budget. We believe that everything we have belongs to God. I do not preach the legalistic tithe. I do not believe it. They called me from the synod office and wanted me to do a stewardship campaign, and I said, "I don't do those." And that is when they told me that my church at Liberty Hill was, per capita giving per member, leading the synod. And I said, "Well, I am real thankful for that, but we have never had a stewardship campaign here, and as long as they meet the budget, we won't. So I don't know how to do them. You are talking to the wrong person."

I do not believe in the legalistic tithe. Ten percent of what you have does not belong to God. You hear that? A hundred percent of what you have belongs to God. God is interested in how you make it, how you spend it, and how much you give to God's work. You know, if I am making $15,000 a year and I am expected to tithe and I got three kids and I am a single parent, what in the world am I going to do? Well, number one, I am going to be eaten up with guilt if my preacher is beating me over the head with that legalistic tithe thing. But suppose I am making $15 million a year, and I feel good about giving a tenth. That is a penance. If I am making $15 million a year, I ought to be able to give at least 30 percent or more. You see what I mean? Why do we want to take one law out of the Old Testament, the tithe law, and make it absolute when we go home after Sunday worship and eat pork and all this other stuff that the Old Testament says not to do. All that we have belongs to God.

IV. Our God Wants Our Thanksgiving—Psalm 50:14-15

In this beautiful psalm passage, God says, "Oh, I don't rebuke your sacrifices, but I don't want them. I don't need them. I don't do that." But what does God say He wants you remember? "I want your thank offering; I want your gratitude; I want your thanksgiving; I want your appreciation."

My most favorite text comes out of Habakkuk, and this is what it says: "Though the fig tree does not bud and there are no grapes on the vine, though the olive crop fails and the fields produce no food, though there are no sheep in the pen and no cattle in the stalls, yet will I rejoice in my God" (Hab. 8:17-18). You think about the thanksgiving you have and I have; it is almost always circumstantial thanksgiving: God, I thank you for this and I thank you for that. No. In times when there is no this or that, we are to be thankful.

CONCLUSION

Years ago in my first little parish, there was a single widowed mother of four. She was almost a day laborer; she had only a little bit better job than that. All four kids were in school. She was in a horrific accident and broke her leg. She got home from the hospital. I made a hospital visit and then a home visit, and at home I was trying to do my feeble, pastoral care at that point, and I said to her, "Well, Ms. Calloway, you know you could have broken your back," because she was telling me how thankful she was, and I thought, *Well you know, she's got a broken leg, but she's thankful she didn't break her back.* And she said, "Gene, if I had broken my back, I'd still be thankful." And then she said to me, "Preacher, let me teach you a lesson. I believe in First Thessalonians when it says in all circumstance give thanks unto God."

In all circumstances. That is what God wants from us. Gratitude, thanksgiving, and praise for the bounty that God has blessed us with, the abundance that God has given us. And it is out of that concept that the understanding, the belief of God's ownership of everything that gratitude best comes. Let us pray.

Thank You, Lord, for these beautiful words from Your scripture that point us to the beautiful creation, Your creation of not only our planetary system but Your creation of us as Your children created in Your image. And then in the progress of revelation, You come to us in Jesus the Christ to teach us just how much You do love us. As Your children, Your creation, we are doubly owned then by Your redemption in Jesus. Help us as Your children to live out gratefully, thankfully, and rejoicingly that we are Yours. In Jesus's name, amen.

NOTES

1. Hazel Felleman, *The Best Loved Poems of the American People* (Garden City, NY: Doubleday & Company, Inc. 1936), 73.

THOUGHT PROVOKERS

I do not literally believe that God wills a bird to die or counts the hairs upon my head.

"Are not two sparrows sold for a penny? Yet not one of them will fall to the ground apart from the will of your Father. And even the very hairs of your head are all numbered" (Matt. 10:29-30 NIV).

CHAPTER 8

I Do Not Take the Bible's Worldview Literally

Sermon Syllabus

Text: Acts 1:1-11; Luke 16:23; Revelation 7:1; Joshua 10:13

CIT: In the biblical period, the worldview was that the Earth was flat, heaven was up, hell was down, and the sun moved.

Thesis: We have a worldview today based upon science and not the literal Bible.

Purpose:
- Major Objective: Doctrinal
- Specific Objective: Through the power of the Holy Spirit, I hope to lead us in interpreting the biblical worldview.

Introduction

Outline:
 I. Heaven Is Not Up—Acts 1:1-11
 II. Hell Is Not Down—Luke 16:23
 III. Earth Is Not Flat—Revelation 7:1
 IV. The Sun Does Not Move—Joshua 10:13

Conclusion

THE WORD OF THE LORD

Revelation 7:1
"After this I saw four angels standing at the four corners of the earth, holding back the four winds of the earth to prevent any wind from blowing on the land or on the sea or on any tree."

Joshua 10:12-14

On the day the Lord gave the Amorites over to Israel, Joshua said to the Lord in the presence of Israel:

"O sun, stand still over Gibeon, O moon, over the Valley of Aijalon."

So the sun stood still, and the moon stopped, till the nation avenged itself on its enemies, as it is written in the Book of Jashar.

The sun stopped in the middle of the sky and delayed going down about a full day. There has never been a day like it before or since, a day when the Lord listened to a man. Surely the Lord was fighting for Israel!

INTRODUCTION

Speaking of worldviews, Webster defines worldview in this fashion: (1) "The overall perspective from which one sees and interprets the world; (2) A collection of beliefs about life and the universe." All of us have a worldview, whether we realize it or not. We hold that view unconsciously or consciously. I think it is crucially important for it to be consciously.

Last week while I was in my cardiologist's waiting room at the heart hospital at Palmetto Richland, I was waiting to see my cardiologist after having had my blood work done. There I sat in this luxurious waiting room in one of the finest heart hospitals in our state that has the most expensive equipment in our state, including every medical gadget relating to the heart known to humankind. I was sitting elbow to elbow with other patients, and a woman to my right answered her phone. I could tell rather quickly that she was talking to an adult daughter who had her own children and was in some kind of trouble.

This mother said to her daughter, "This is urgent! You get a box of table salt and go outside and you walk around your house counterclockwise three times sprinkling that salt. It is crucial that you protect your family. You go do this immediately." I was just deeply impressed by the contrast of our worldviews. There we were, seated in the most medically advanced facility in and around us, and I didn't know what kind of protection she was talking about, but she said to her daughter, "You must protect your home and family, and this is the way you do it." What was her worldview? Her worldview was magical and deeply superstitious.

My mama had a worldview. I don't know how many times I heard her say this when we were going off or going out, I mean beginning with little children all the way up. She would catch us by the hand—somewhere along the way she had read the book of Job—and she would pray, "God, build a hedge around these boys" or "Build a hedge of Your protection around Gene." I remember that after I got old enough and read the book of Job myself and knew the story, I wanted to say to her, "But, Mama, God sicced the devil on Job, and he lost everything," but I knew better than to say that to her. I remember as a little child I wanted to say to her when she prayed that for me, "You should have prayed to God to build a hedge around our daddy, who died at forty-two," but I knew better than to say that also. But that was her worldview. All of us have one.

I. Heaven Is Not Up—Acts 1:1-11

Our worldviews come from what we experience as children and as young adults. That worldview does not cease to be in process of being formed and altered and changed. We can have a biblical worldview without adopting the worldview that is literally presented in the Bible. Their worldview was that heaven was up and hell was down. Their world was three tiered with hell below, heaven above, and us walking on the middle plain that was flat with four corners. You heard me read it. And that was their cosmic worldview.

Think about it. If you were Neanderthal man or woman standing on a beach and all you know is this one little local place. And you look out over that horizon, and everything about you says that it just *poof*. "I can see it. I can see where it goes *poof.* I can see where it drops off." And it may be that you grow some in your understanding to a point where you build a little boat and paddle there to look and see where it just goes *poof.* You get there, and you say, "Well, I can still see a little farther, but I can see that it just drops off." And everything about your experience tells you that the sun came up in the east, and it moved, all day long it moved, until it settled and went out of sight in the west. There is nothing about your experience that says what you are standing on is moving. Your experience is not that the sun is standing still and what you are standing on is turning. There is nothing about your experience that tells you that.

Our worldviews are developed out of our experiences—what we experience personally and what we experience culturally. And you put with that, as Neanderthal man continues to evolve, where the scriptures were developed and where they told us we came from. That God created, and this is what God created. There were those Neanderthals who thought everything up there was bright and shiny and wonderful and good. Our light comes from up there. Our sun, our heat comes from up there to grow our food and warm our backs. The fresh rain comes from up there. So everything up there must be wonderful and good.

It is like James and his book when he says all good gifts come from where? From above, from the father of what? The father of lights (James 1:17). And if that Neanderthal man is living anywhere around a volcano and sees that horrible fire belching up from the bowels of the Earth, then what is below? It can't be good. He smells the stink of the sulfur that comes from that volcanic overflow. What is down there cannot be good. And you can bet if he was anywhere around a cave and walked into it, to see the darkness and feel the moist air and wipe the spider webs off his face and see the crawly things on the floor caused his whole experience to say everything down there was not good. It was dark and dismal. And names were developed. Heaven was a place of wonderful, light-giving everything, and hell became the place of darkness, fear, punishment, and death. And it was out of that experience that the people of the biblical period formed the worldview that heaven was up, hell was down, and this is where we live. Everything good is up there, and everything bad is down there.

II. Hell Is Not Down—Luke 16:23

We do not have to adopt those four things to have a biblical worldview. We can have a biblical worldview through interpreting the scriptures and not taking them literally. My interpretation of heaven is that I do not need a place. My spirit does not need a place. My spirit is beyond space and time. I have no need of gold streets upon which to walk. I have no need of pearly gates to look at. My spirit does not need any of that. What my spirit longs for is the connection, the fellowship, the relationship to the spiritual God who created me as spirit. But out of their experience, John wanted to say, "Let me tell you about a place beyond any beauty you have ever seen, beyond any riches you have every imaged." And out of John's only tool, which is his language, he talks about the pearly gates of heaven and the sapphire walls, and if you want to believe that, that is fine and well. You may. I don't need to. My spirit does not need a place. And with all the wonderful things coming from up there, Jesus accommodated their understanding. And when He left them, "He went up" (Acts 1:9; Luke 24:51).

It was also out of their language, which was their only tool, that they spoke about a place that was so horrible that if we were ungodly and rejected God, we would spend an eternity in this place. The most horrible thing they could think of was to be burned, and the most horrible thing in their experience was the Valley of Gehenna, the garbage dump outside Jerusalem that was Jesus's word for hell. And when He talked about hell, He talked about Gehenna, that place where the worms and maggots never stopped moving and the fire never stopped burning and the stench never stopped coming up. They used the only thing they had—their experiences. And their experiences were limited by language, and they shared it with us.

III. Earth Is Not Flat—Revelation 7:1

We do not have to take the scriptures literally to take them reverently, seriously, and respectfully. In fact, when I do not take them literally, I can take them more seriously, more reverently, and more respectfully. When I take them interpretably, I don't get caught up wrestling with the poem of Genesis. It's a poem. I don't get caught up in the literalism of Joshua asking God to make the sun stand still and the Bible saying the sun stands still when it can't do that because it never moved to begin with.

I said to a group of preachers one time that God couldn't make the sun stand still because it already was standing still, and one of the preachers said to me, "God can do anything God wants to do." I said, "No, God can't. You can't make something stop moving that is not moving." Can you do that?

IV. THE SUN DOES NOT MOVE—JOSHUA 10:13

When one takes seriously that Israel had a worldview that was shaped by their culture, shaped by their experience, shaped by what they believed and that they put it down. Therefore, we don't have to take it literally. In fact, it was never meant to be taken literally. They understood when they were speaking metaphorically, and they understood when they were speaking historical fact. We have lost that. We have lost the dualistic concept of "mythos and logos" because of this immense time span between us.[1]

I think, for me, I take it much more seriously when I impose upon myself the responsibility of interpreting the scriptures in a way that feeds my life and instructs my soul. I have a worldview, but it does not incorporate these: heaven is up, hell is down, and the sun moves. My worldview is very simple. There are seven statements, and most of them are in 1 Corinthians 15:3-8.

My worldview is this: God created all that there is. And this creator, God, out of the benevolent love for us, sent Jesus, who died for my sins, was buried for three days, resurrected out of that tomb, is alive today, and out of that aliveness and that resurrection, after my death, I will follow. That is my worldview. That is what Paul said in Corinthians. He said to them,

". . . what I received I passed on to you as of first importance: that Christ died for our sins according to the Scriptures, that he was buried, that he was raised on the third day according to the Scriptures, and that he appeared to Peter, and then to the Twelve." (1 Cor.15:3-5)

CONCLUSION

This past summer has been painful in some ways because of the criticism, but it has been joyful in other ways. I have had people, at least one, say to me, "I don't see how you claim to be a Christian believing what you believe." I said, "That's okay. I understand. I understand why you can't understand that I am a Christian." I had another person say to me, "You are a Christian; you just are not a good one." And that is okay too. And I remember saying to one dear sweet fellow, "I am a Christian, but I am a pragmatic Christian," meaning my faith has to work, and if it doesn't work, what good is it? It's not functional. If it doesn't make me a better person, if it doesn't help me, what good is it? For me it has to work; it has to be real. I hope and pray that this summer has been helpful to your faith and not disastrous. Here is the essence of worldview that I embrace: Christ died for our sins, was buried, resurrected on the third day, and is alive to greet us in our resurrection. That is my worldview. Amen.

NOTES

1. Karen Armstrong, *The Battle for God*. (New York: Alfred A. Knope, 2000), IX-XVI.

THOUGHT PROVOKERS

I do not take literally the law that says a rebellious child should be stoned to death.

> If someone has a stubborn and rebellious son who does not obey his father and mother and will not listen to them when they discipline him, his father and mother shall take hold of him and bring him to the elders at the gate of his town. They shall say to the elders, "This son of ours is stubborn and rebellious. He will not obey us. He is a glutton and a drunkard." Then all the men of his town are to stone him to death. You must purge the evil from among you. All Israel will hear of it and be afraid. (Deut. 21:18-21 NIV)

CHAPTER 9

I TAKE SERIOUSLY THE BIBLE'S ADMONITION TO BE LOVE SLAVES

SERMON SYLLABUS

Text: Philippians 2:1-11

CIT: Jesus was a love slave in relationship to God.

Thesis: As Christians we are encouraged to have Jesus's attitude of being God's love slave.

Purpose:
- Major Objective: Supportive
- Specific Objective: Through the power of the Holy Spirit, I hope to lead each of us in being lovingly devoted to God.

Introduction

Outline:
I. Jesus Is Our Example of God's Love Slave—Philippians 2:6-7; John 13:1-17
II. We Are to Follow Jesus's Example—Philippians 2:1-2 & 5.
III. Loving God Is Loving Other People—Philippians 2:3-4; James 1:26-27; 3:9-12; 2:8; John 13:34; Galatians 5:14; Mark 12:29-31

Conclusion

THE WORD OF THE LORD

Philippians 2:1-11

If you have any encouragement from being united with Christ, if any comfort from his love, if any fellowship with the Spirit, if any tenderness and compassion, then make my joy complete by being like-minded, having the same love, being one in spirit and purpose. Do nothing out of selfish ambition or vain conceit, but in humility consider others better than yourselves. Each of you should look not only to your own interests, but also to the interests of others.

Your attitude should be the same as that of Christ Jesus:

Who, being in very nature God, did not consider equality with God something to be grasped, but made himself nothing, taking the very nature of a servant, being made in human likeness. And being found in appearance as a man, he humbled himself and became obedient to death—even death on a cross! Therefore God exalted him to the highest place and gave him the name that is above every name, that at the name of Jesus every knee should bow, in heaven and on earth and under the earth, and every tongue confess that Jesus Christ is Lord, to the glory of God the Father.

INTRODUCTION

A few weeks ago I was told that I could not take Jesus seriously if I did not take his virgin birth literally. And I said to the person, "Thank you for being so assured of what I can do or cannot do." Isn't that wonderful when people tell you that? They tell you what you can do and what you can't do, and sometimes they tell you where you can go or where you can't go. And sometimes they tell you what you can think and what you can't think. And I said to him, "I can take Jesus as seriously as I choose to take Jesus and in any way I choose to take Jesus. I do not have to comply with your way of thinking." But I would say that this text and my speaking on it need to be placed with the sermon of the seriousness with which I take Jesus's identity. I do take Jesus's identity very seriously and very theologically, but I do not take his virgin birth literally. But that is for a later sermon, so I hope you will come back without a bag of stones, please.

I. JESUS IS OUR EXAMPLE OF GOD'S LOVE SLAVE—PHILIPPIANS 2:6-7; JOHN 13:1-17

Paul says in this text that our thinking should be compatible with the thinking of Jesus. Twice he says this to us. In Phil. 2:2, he says, "Be like-minded." And he uses the Greek word, which is a noun, *Nous,* which means simple mind. And in 1 Corinthians 8:9, the scriptures tell us that we have the mind of Christ. But in verse 5, Paul uses a different word. He does not use the Greek word *Nous*; he uses the Greek verb *Phoneo,* which is best translated in our text just like it is "attitude" or "thought." Now, in the King James, it still uses the word *mind*. Let this mind be in you. But that is not the most accurate. It is *Phoneo,* which is a verb.

So the scripture is saying that as his followers, we are to have his thoughts reproduced in us because we have within us the mind of Christ, the Spirit of Christ, the Holy Spirit—however you want to say that. And with the Spirit being within us, we then are capable of reproducing Jesus's thoughts. What is the thought Paul is encouraging us to reproduce? That is the real key to this text. It says that Jesus, not grasping equality with God because He, being fully God, laid aside the splendor and glory of heaven, took upon Him humanity, and came to live among us in the form of a servant. That is a fascinating Greek word. The word is *Doulos,* and it means slave. But not just any slave; it is a "love slave."

In Jesus's day, slavery abounded. A Jewish person could be enslaved for lots of reasons. But in the year of jubilee, which was the seventh year, if it was a Jewish slave, he or she had to be freed. If it was a foreign person, he or she could be kept for generations. Foreign slaves did not have to be freed in the seventh year of jubilee. But they often were, for whatever reason. And often when owners released the Jewish slaves, in our terminology today we would say that that slave had become "institutionalized," but I think it is much deeper than that. The slave would say to the master, "I don't have anywhere else to go. I don't want to go anywhere else. I love it here. You have treated me respectfully and lovingly, and I don't want to go anywhere else." In other words, "I will choose to take my freedom and keep it here." When a slave did that, he or she was taken and a rather large hole was punched into his or her earlobe, and then when that slave was seen publicly, the hole in his or her ear indicated that this was a *Doulos*, a slave who was slave to his or her master out of love, not slavery. He or she had been set free.

You have your freedom, but in your freedom you have chosen to stay in this household with this master. But to let everyone else know, the slaves of that day took that hole punch and punched a rather large hole in their earlobes, and the holes were noticeable and often worn with great pride. That is the word that is used here for Jesus. It says Jesus became God's love slave. Jesus did what He did out of absolute freedom and personal liberty in coming and laying apart the glory and splendor of heaven and coming to be one of us and live in fashion as a servant.

II. We Are to Follow Jesus's Example—Philippians 2:1-2 & 5

I could pick several passages, but I will only pick one. Remember that magnificent story in the Gospel of John the thirteenth chapter? It is the passion week, the last week. They are in the upper room. They have had the communion meal, and Jesus takes a towel puts it around him and gets a basin of water and starts washing the disciples' feet. At the conclusion of that lowly servant's task, Jesus says, "As I have been servant to you, you are to be servants to others. For in the kingdom of God, the first is last and the last is first." This magnificent picture of Jesus's servanthood is *Doulos*. A love slave to God. And then Paul takes that picture and says to us that as followers of our Lord, we are to be a *Doulos*, a love slave.

I hope you can take in just a little bit of what that means. You have been set free from your sins, your mistakes; you are set free from your sins and your mistakes. You are free from the obligations. You are free from the law. You have been justified. That word means just as if you had never sinned. All those rich words of being redeemed were bought with a price. Think about that! You have been set free, and you have been given one obligation. You have been given one responsibility. One. That is all. And that one responsibility is to be what Jesus was—a *Doulos*, a love slave. You are free, but you are under a love obligation. You are free, forgiven, at liberty, set free, and one response is called from you, and that is to love.

And do you know what Jesus did with that? In the synoptic Gospels—all of them recorded the event—this lawyer comes to Jesus and says, "We have debated this for years. There are all kinds of parties that have taken a stake at what they believe. What is the greatest commandment?" And Jesus said, "Here it is." Remember it? Jesus said, "Thou shalt love the Lord thy God with all thy heart, mind, and spirit," and the way you do that, Jesus said, is thou shalt love thy neighbor as thyself.

III. Loving God Is Loving Other People—Philippians 2:3-4; James 1:26-27; 3:9-12; 2:8; John 13:34; Galatians 5:14; Mark 12:29-31

My favorite president, Abraham Lincoln, played with the Presbyterians, courted the Presbyterians, and had a Presbyterian minister preach his children's funerals. He had lots of losses, but he never joined a Presbyterian church. In fact, he never joined any church. He had more scripture in his speeches than any president before him or after him. He invoked God in his speeches more than any president before him or after him and was criticized greatly for not being a church member, and this is what he said: "When I find a church that has one creed and one creed only, when I find a church and they have this nailed over their door, this one thing, I will join it. No other creed, no other covenant, no other statement, just this one: thou shalt love the Lord thy God with all thy heart, soul, mind, and body, and thou shalt love thy neighbor as thyself. When I find that church, I will join it." [1]

When they buried him, he had not found that church. Therefore, he was not a church member at any point or time in his life. But was he theologically on-target? Absolutely! Absolutely! That is what Jesus says, and that is what the scriptures tell us. In Galatians 5:14, it says, "Everything can be summed up in one command: thou shalt love thy neighbor as thyself."

And how many times have I said to you, and it bears repeating, that I personally do not know how to love God in any other way than loving the likes of you people. I don't know how to do it. In fact, James, half-brother of Jesus, said out of one side of your mouth you talk about how much you love God and out of the other side of your mouth you cuss human beings who are created in the image of God. You can't do that, James said. You do not take figs and prunes off the same bush. You do not take salt water and fresh water out of the same stream. You can't spit forth "I love God" out of one side of your mouth and "I hate my neighbor" out of the other side of your mouth. Who is in God's image? Who is the only representation of God on this Earth?

So we have been set free, forgiven. Freed from slavery to our sin, to our guilt, to our remorse, and you are free to abound in liberty with one responsibility, one obligation, and that is to love each other as I have loved you. That is what Jesus said is the new commandment. You think about the times you may have said, "Well, I just hate so and so." Or you have heard someone say, "Oh, I just hate her" or "I hate him." That is treading on thin ice. James said you cannot do that. You cannot say down on your knees beside your bed, "Oh God, I love you so, but that ***** down the street, I hate." Can't do it.

You know one of the reasons marriages are so stuck in unforgiveness is that we do not pray for each other. We don't call each other's name before God's throne of grace. I will tell you why we don't, and I will tell you how it would be. You cannot pray with clenched teeth and fists, "Lord, bless her. Just bless her." You can't do it. You have to let that stuff go. You have to let it go. And when you let it go, you are living what Jesus call us to live. We are reproducing that life of *Doulos*, a love slave, here on this Earth.

CONCLUSION

The following is a beautiful excerpt from *Poem in Prose*. In a poem by <u>Ivan S. Turgenev</u>, he says these words:

The Sparrow

I was returning from hunting, and walking along an avenue of the garden, my dog running in front of me.

Suddenly he took shorter steps, and began to steal along as though tracking game.

I looked along the avenue, and saw a young sparrow, with yellow about its beak and down on its head. It had fallen out of the nest (the wind was violently shaking the birch-trees in the avenue) and sat unable to move, helplessly flapping its half-grown wings.

My dog was slowly approaching it, when, suddenly darting down from a tree close by, an old dark-throated sparrow fell like a stone right before his nose, and all ruffled up, terrified, with despairing and pitiful cheeps, it flung itself twice towards the open jaws of shining teeth.

It sprang to save; it cast itself before its nestling . . . but all its tiny body was shaking with terror; its note was harsh and strange. Swooning with fear, it offered itself up!

What a huge monster must the dog have seemed to it! And yet it could not stay on its high branch out of danger. . . . A force stronger than its will flung it down.

My Trésor stood still, drew back. . . . Clearly he too recognized this force.

I hastened to call off the disconcerted dog, and went away, full of reverence.

Yes; do not laugh. I felt reverence for that tiny heroic bird, for its impulse of love.

Love, I thought, is stronger than death or the fear of death. Only by it, by love, life holds together and advances.[1]

I stand in awe of God's gracious love for us, and I stand in awe of our own unworthiness. But being recipients of that awesome gracious love, we are then compelled to live it out. Let us do so. Let us pray.

Lord Jesus, thank You that like a mama sparrow You couldn't stay perched above watching Your children, Your creation flounder in sin and unforgiveness. But You flung Yourself from the glories of heaven to come and live among us as an example and died as a sacrifice. And You have said to us as Your people just consider one thing: that you love each other as I have loved you. Help us to do so in Your power. In Jesus's name, amen.

NOTES

1. William J. Wolf, *The Almost Chosen People* (New York: Doubleday & Company Inc., 1959), 105-106

2. Ivan S. Turgenev, "The Sparrow" (http://www.online-literature.com/turgenev/2707, April 1878) (I accessed the site, 12-18-2012)

THOUGHT PROVOKERS

I do not take literally the law that people who worship differently than me should be destroyed.

> When the LORD your God brings you into the land you are entering to possess and drives out before you many nations—the Hitties, Girgashites, Amorites, Canaanites, Perizzites, Hivites, and Jebusites, seven nations larger and stronger than you, and when the LORD your God has delivered them over to you and you have defeated the, then you must destroy them totally. Make no treaty with them, and show them no mercy. Do not intermarry with them. Do not give your daughters to their sons or take their daughters for your sons, for they will turn you children away from following me to serve other gods, and the LORD's anger will burn against you and will quickly destroy you. This is what you are to do to them: Break down their altars, smash their sacred stones, cut down their Asherah poles and burn their idols in the firs. For you are a people holy to the LORD your God. The LORD your God has chosen you out of all the peoples on the face of the earth to be his people, his treasured possession. (Deut. 7:1-6)

CHAPTER 10

I Do Not Take Literally the Bible's Admonition to Slaves

Sermon Syllabus

Text: Ephesians 6:5-9; Colossians 3:22-25; 1 Timothy 6:1-2; Titus 2:9-10; 1 Peter 2:18-21 (read also the Letter to Philemon)

CIT: The Bible taught slaves to be obedient to their masters in everything.

Thesis: To take the Bible literally is to take slavery as a God-ordained institution.

Purpose
- Major Objective: Ethical/Actional
- Specific Objective: Through the power of the Holy Spirit, I hope to lead each of us in affirming the freedom of all people.

Introduction

Outline:
I. The Bible Admonishes Slaves to Be Obedient, Respectful, and Reverent Toward Their Masters Even When Ill-Treated.
II. The Bible Has Paul Sending the Slave Onesimus Back to His Master, Philemon
III. The World Universally and Unequivocally Rejects the Owning of One Person by Another Person.

Conclusion

THE WORD OF THE LORD

Ephesians 6:5-9

> Slaves, obey your earthly masters with respect and fear, and with sincerity of heart, just as you would obey Christ. Obey them not only to win their favor when their eye is on you, but as slaves of Christ, doing the will of God from your heart. Serve wholeheartedly, as if you were serving the Lord, not people, because you know that the Lord will reward each one for whatever good they do, whether they are slave or free. And masters, treat your slaves in the same way. Do not threaten them, since you know that he who is both their Master and yours is in heaven, and there is no favoritism with him.

Colossians 3:22-25

> Slaves, obey your earthly masters in everything; and do it, not only when their eye is on you and to curry their favor, but with sincerity of heart and reverence for the Lord. Whatever you do, work at it with all your heart, as working for the Lord, not for human masters, since you know that you will receive an inheritance from the Lord as a reward. It is the Lord Christ you are serving. Anyone who does wrong will be repaid for their wrongs, and there is no favoritism.

I Timothy 6:1-2

> All who are under the yoke of slavery should consider their masters worthy of full respect, so that God's name and our teaching may not be slandered. Those who have believing masters should not show them disrespect just because they are fellow believers. Instead, they should serve them even better because their masters are dear to them as fellow believers and are devoted to the welfare of their slaves. These are the things you are to teach and urge on them.

Titus 2:9-10

> "Teach slaves to be subject to their masters in everything, to try to please them, not to talk back to them, and not to steal from them,

but to show that they can be fully trusted, so that in every way they will make the teaching about God our Savior attractive."

1 Peter 2:18-21

Slaves, in reverent fear of God submit yourselves to your masters, not only to those who are good and considerate, but also to those who are harsh. For it is commendable if someone bears up under the pain of unjust suffering because they are conscious of God. But how is it to your credit if you receive a beating for doing wrong and endure it? But if you suffer for doing good and you endure it, this is commendable before God. To this you were called, because Christ suffered for you, leaving you an example, that you should follow in his steps.

INTRODUCTION

I cannot take these words about slavery literally without believing in slavery. If I take these words literally, I have no other choice than to believe in the institution of slavery. That is exactly the way our forefathers felt. Let me read a long excerpt from a sermon that I researched. I could have chosen a sermon that was preached in my historical pulpit at Liberty Hill, but I have used it before in the church. But in my research, I found ample sermons to use. Trust me. This one comes from March 1849, preached in Columbia, South Carolina, by a Presbyterian minister. It is recorded in the second volume of the *Presbyterian Review*, published in March 1849. Here is part of his words, and I quote:

> In the tenth commandment, graven with God's finger on marble, we find the solemn, divine recognition of rights of property. Thou shalt not covet anything that is thy neighbor's. Do you find yourself without things? That is poor. See that you do not even wish in your heart to have your neighbor's things however abundantly the sovereign but righteous Lord of all has bestowed them upon him in contrast with yourself. The same divine commandments sanctions even the right of property in human beings and thus gives warrant to our rights of authority as slave holders. The lawgiver says thou shalt not covet thy neighbor's

man slave nor his maid slave nor his ox nor his ass nor anything that is thy neighbor's. Does the almighty God then count slaves as human cattle? Is a slave a mere thing? Far from it. He is an immortal man but he has a human master by God's appointment and that master has right of property over him, has a right in his service which no other man can innocently covet. No, the slave himself must not covet or take what belongs not to himself. The scriptures then did not originate the idea that all men simply from the fact of being a man has a natural right to an equal amount of property or an equal share of personal liberty. The northerner says slavery is antichristian and always and everywhere sinful. That cannot be antichristian however which Christ and the apostles never condemned. And slavery must be just left alone to stand upon the same footing with any other inequality of condition until some higher revelations in the Bible shall show forth that the revelation itself is inconsistent with the moral nature of man and deprives him of his ethic character. In other words, if he cannot truly worship God. Christianity unquestionably sanctions slavery. Christianity also civilizes the slave. Christianity improves the slave in all parts of its character. You of the north should not abolish that which must be and ought to be fortified and confirmed. The master's authority must not be withdrawn. Our system of slavery is a civilizer and a Christianizer. We must leave it for God to remove when His time comes. Meanwhile, we must maintain it always administering it in accordance to the love of the apostle bless be to God.[1]

I hope that insulted your sensitivity. It surely does mine. Preacher, are you saying that the Bible's admonition to slaves instituted slavery? No. We have pictographs on cave walls long before written history, depicting one tribe going to another tribe and capturing people and bringing them home into servitude, primarily women, dragging them by their hair. Slavery has existed since the dawn of humankind. It existed prior to written history.

So these words that I just read to you and the words of Leviticus chapter 25 did not originate slavery; neither did it cause it. Did it continue to support it? Absolutely! Did our forefathers, especially in the South, take the scriptures and browbeat their slaves and browbeat the people up north, saying it was God's ordained institution? Absolutely! And research shows that there are thousands of sermons preached throughout the South that took these words literally and applied them literally. Could these words have been used in a different way? Absolutely, and they were by some, as we will see later.

I. The Bible Admonishes Slaves to Be Obedient, Respectful, and Reverent Toward Their Masters Even When Ill-Treated

In Jesus's day, Josephus, the Jewish historian, tells us that under the rule of the Roman Empire there were about sixty million slaves. When Rome conquered a nation, they simply enslaved them. Sixty million. The Code of Hammurabi is a law code that dates 1760 BC, which by the way contains six of our ten commandments and predates Moses's Ten Commandments by several hundred years. The Code of Hammurabi spoke to the treatment of slaves, so it had always been around. In an 1860 U.S. census, there were 393,975 U.S. citizens who owned slaves. That was 8 percent. There were 3,950,528 slaves in America, the first one being imported in 1619. We have a long sordid history with slaves. Liberty Hill at one time had about three hundred slaves working in the cotton fields, raising cotton to send down the Wateree River to Charleston to be sent to the motherland. Our balcony in our church was designed for slaves. In the origin of the building, there was an outside stairwell so the slaves did not enter the downstairs sanctuary to get to their segregated balcony upstairs.

Aristotle wrote, "A slave is a living tool just as any tool is an inanimate object." Vero wrote, "The slave is no better than a beast who happens to have a voice." Gaius the Roman lawyer wrote, "It is universally accepted that the master possess the power of life and death over the slaves."[2] It is my contention this morning and throughout this summer that many of our past mistakes, our current mistakes, and our future mistakes in relationship to scripture could be avoided if we did not take the scripture literally but rather if we took it interpretively, interpreting the passages first and foremost within their context. And the context in which this was written was that at the time, slavery was universally accepted and universally employed. We must simply interpret these verses of scripture as addressing an institution not ordained by God.

If I were a slave and God placed me in that position, then could I be an obedient slave? I guess some could. Gene Rollins could not. I would be a hostile life taker of my master at my first chance. That is the anger that would be there if I believed God had placed me in that position. When one believes the ultimate authority in life has done you in, the lesser authorities of life mean nothing. I have been there. Do you ever wonder why it is that per capita the highest percentage of our inmates, not just in South Carolina but in the United States, are professing Christians? Do you ever wonder about that? No, Gene, we don't wonder about that. We pay you to wonder about that. You have never asked why. Why is it that so many professing Christians are criminals who wind up in institutions? Is that the Christian message? No. We get all tangled up unconsciously and psychically with what God is doing to us. When you can lash out at God for doing it to you, you can lash out at anyone.

There was a time in my life when a policeman or a teacher meant nothing to me. I answered to no authority because I was thumbing my nose at the highest authority for killing my father. That goes on within us unconsciously. Raging out. And that is one of the primary factors and reasons that criminal institutions today per capita have more professing Christians than anyone else. More professing Christians than non-Christians, not just other denominations. There is one reason for that.

If we take the scriptures interpretively, they are addressing a situation that was simply going on. They were not supporting it, they were not encouraging it, they were not saying go out and own slaves. Paul was simply addressing a situation that existed. Personally, I wish he had addressed it differently.

II. The Bible Has Paul Sending the Slave Onesimus Back to His Master, Philemon

Two books are the saddest books in the Bible to me. The first book is Jonah in the Old Testament because Jonah won't go to these people because they are non-Jewish, and he wants them damned to hell anyway. He doesn't want them to repent, so he won't go preach to them. Sad.

The second book is Philemon. I know you haven't read it. It is just one chapter. Paul writes back to his friend Philemon, who has a house church, and he says to Philemon, "Your runaway slave, Onesimus, is with me." Although he never says "slave," we know because of what he says and because the slave's name, Onesimus, means useful, and 70 percent of the slaves then were renamed Onesimus because they were useful. I could wish Paul had written back to Philemon and said, "Onesimus has become a believer. He is my right arm." In fact, Paul says, "He is my heart, and I am saying to you, brother, that he is your brother and your equal." He hints at that, but then he sends Onesimus back to his master and tells him to go back into servitude. He does tell Philemon to treat him well and said that if Onesimus owed Philemon anything (which suggests he probably stole something to make his escape), "I will pay you back. Don't worry about it." I wish he had just set him free and said the gospel says there are no slaves. But he didn't.

III. The World Universally and Unequivocally Rejects the Owning of One Person by Another Person

Listen to this next statement. The world today universally and unequivocally rejects slavery as inhumane, immoral, and unethical. There is not a nation on Mother Earth that does not have written political statements to that effect. Yet the latest research I have found says we are approaching 20 million slaves in the world today. Eighteen percent of them are sex slaves involved in sex trafficking. When are we going to come to universally believe that we are created in the image of God, all of us, and resoundly reject that any one image of God could own another image of God? When can we come to that place? I pray soon.

But I must say that in these same scriptures, there are the seeds for emancipation. I hope you noticed it twice in Ephesians 6:8-9—"With God there is no favoritism"—and the Colossians 3:25 passage that states there is no favoritism. There is that seed planted deep in the unconscious of humankind that God almighty does not play favorites. God almighty does not have favorites. This is a hard lesson for Peter in the tenth chapter of Acts. In fact, it is so hard that God has to use hypnosis to help him out. In the tenth chapter of Acts, Peter is up on the rooftop, taking a nap before dinner (the roofs were flat), and he had a dream. He saw this sheet coming down with all these non-Jewish animals on it—you know, animals with hoofs, pigs, snakes, good old crayfish, shrimp, lobster, all that kind of stuff—and the voice said, "Peter, kill and eat." And Peter said, "I don't eat that unclean stuff." And the voice said, "Do not you call unclean what I have made clean." Not once but three times he saw and heard that.

Stating something three times is a classical thing in hypnosis today. Whatever you are going to suggest, you suggest it three times. Peter came out of that trance, and a Gentile knocked at the door. (Jews had nothing to do with Gentiles; they were Gentile dogs.) He went to the door, and this Gentile said, "We are having a prayer meeting at my house and the Spirit of God said come to this place and get Peter to come pray and talk to us." Peter said, "Ah-ha," a gestalt moment, an epiphany. It didn't have anything to do with food, and Peter said, "While in a trance I saw a vision [best definition of hypnosis you will ever read], and the voice said to me, 'God does not have favorites.'"

Had that not happened, there would be no church today. The Christian movement would have died as a little Jewish sect. That encounter made it possible for the church to broaden and include everyone. Just like Paul said in Galatians that we are one—male, female, Jew, Greek, bonded, and free. We are all one in Christ Jesus. Paul also said in Galatians chapter five, "Christ has set us free. Let us stand firm in that freedom and let us not be brought back into the bondage of slavery." What Paul was talking about that had enslaved them was legalism. I want to change his word today. Christ has set us free. Stand firm then in your freedom and do not be brought back into the bondage of literalism of the scriptures. Let them in the Spirit of God set you free.

CONCLUSION

I had hoped that Gene would sing one of those wonderful old spirituals, but he let me down. We have this belief that all of those black spirituals were happy. We have this belief of the happy slaves. Do not believe that. Here is one I came up with in my research:

> Before I'd be a slave I'd be buried in my grave
> And go home to my Lord and be saved.
> Oh what preaching over me oh what preaching over me
> Before I be a slave, I be buried in my grave.
> Oh what moaning over me oh what moaning over me
> Oh what singing shoutin moaning over me

For before I be a slave I be buried in my grave
And there will be singing there will be moaning over me.[2]

Hallelujah. Let us pray. Lord Jesus, thank You that You have set us free in Christ Jesus who came and lived and died that everyone, everyone might experience Your love and Your forgiveness. Thank you, O God, for giving us the minds, the intellects that You have given us. Thank you for this treasure of scripture that Your Holy Spirit has preserved and help us to use it intelligently to free us in Christ Jesus. In Jesus's name, amen.

Notes

1. S. B. Treat, "Human Rights and Slavery," in *Southern Presbyterian Review*, vol. 11 (March 1849).
2. Wikipedia, Last modified December 17, 2012. http://en.wikipedia.org/wiki/styleguide
3. William E. Barton, *Old Plantation Hymns* (1899).

THOUGHT PROVOKERS

I do not take literally that a woman should keep her mouth shut in church.

"For God is not a God of disorder but of peace—as in all the congregations of the Lord's people. Women should remain silent in the churches. They are not allowed to speak, but must be in submission, as the law says. If they want to inquire about something, they should ask their own husbands at home; for it is disgraceful for a woman to speak in the church" (1 Cor. 14:33-35 NIV).

CHAPTER 11

I TAKE SERIOUSLY THE BIBLE'S EQUALITY OF ALL PEOPLE

SERMON SYLLABUS

Text: Genesis 1:27; Leviticus 19:15; Galatians 3:26-29

CIT: God always had a plan for inclusion of all people in God's love.

Thesis: God is the God of whosoever will may come (Rev. 22:17).

Purpose:
- Major Objective: Doctrinal
- Specific Objective: Through the power of the Holy Spirit, I hope to lead each of us in affirming God's inclusive love.

Introduction

Outline:
- I. God Is Impartial According to Creation of All Humankind—Genesis 1:27; 2:20
- II. God Is Impartial According to Ethnicity—Acts 10:34-35; Romans 10:12; Galatians 2:6
- III. God Is Impartial According to Gender—Galatians 3:26-29
- IV. God Is Impartial According to Social Standing—Job 34:19; James 2:1-10

Conclusion

THE WORD OF THE LORD

Genesis 1:27
"So God created mankind in his own image, in the image of God he created them; male and female he created them."

Leviticus 19:15
"Do not pervert justice; do not show partiality to the poor or favoritism to the great, but judge your neighbor fairly."

Galatians 3:26-29
"So in Christ Jesus you are all children of God through faith, for all of you who were baptized into Christ have clothed yourselves with Christ. There is neither Jew nor Gentile, neither slave nor free, nor is there male and female, for you are all one in Christ Jesus. If you belong to Christ, then you are Abraham's seed, and heirs according to the promise."

INTRODUCTION

Our Declaration of Independence, which I believe to be one of the most profound documents ever written, says: "We hold these truths to be self-evident, that all men are created equal." Thomas Jefferson did not write those words. Thomas Jefferson wrote, "We hold these truths to be sacred and undeniable." He turned it over to Benjamin Franklin for his editing and suggestions, and it was Benjamin Franklin who wrote the word *self-evident*. We hold these truths to be self-evident . . . I like Jefferson's translation better: "We hold these truths to be sacred and undeniable."

For what our forefathers meant was that all white men were equal. We later really had to struggle with that because in this country when those words were written, the black man did not have equality; the red man did not have equality; and the female gender did not have equality. What our forefathers meant, to their admission, was that white males are equal. It took some bloodshed and some struggles for that to become clear.

In 1948, the Universal Declaration of Human Rights, which Teddy Roosevelt had a big part in, said these words: "All human beings are born free and equal in dignity and in rights." Three things surfaced from that declaration that cut across every boundary: all of humankind is equal in

(1) freedom, (2) dignity, and (3) rights. That is the core of liberty. There is no liberty without equality. There is no democracy without universal equality within that democracy.

I. GOD IS IMPARTIAL ACCORDING TO CREATION OF ALL HUMANKIND—GENESIS 1:27; 2:20

A Yiddish, which is a Jewish proverb, says, "Everyone is kneaded out of the same dough. We are just baked in different ovens." There is a lot of truth in that. We all came over in many different ships, but we are all in the same boat. Right? All of us. This, I believe, is crucial in our understanding, and I take seriously these scriptures when they lay out from God's perspective that equality.

In the first creation story, and you know there are two in the first chapter of Genesis, the scripture says, "God said let us create humankind after our likeness in our image let them have dominion over everything." (Gen. 1:26)And it says that God created them male and female. That is the first creation story. So we have in that first creation story God creating the human race male and female in God's image. The second creation story is the Adam and Eve creation story. And the first time *Adam* is used is in Genesis 2:20: "So the man gave names to all the livestock, birds of the air, beasts of the field. But for Adam there was no suitable helper found." The word *Adam* in English is a transliteration of the Hebrew word *Adom*. Transliterate means that when you are translating from one language to another, you do not have an equivalent to the original word in the second language. We did that with *baptize*. We did not have an English word *baptize*. The Greek word was *baptizo*, so we took *baptizo*, transliterated it, and created the word *baptize*.

Adom is the Hebrew word for "men." Hello, you with me? Did you hear what I just said? I said that the Bible says God created *Adom*, which is the Hebrew word for "men." I personally, not that you have to—I don't ever care whether you agree with me or not, if that makes any difference—but I personally do not believe that humankind originated from two people, Adam and Eve. The geneticists, the DNA folks, tell us that with the human diversity we have today in the gene pool and in the DNA pool, if we started from two people, it would have taken at least 10 billion years for that kind of genetic diversity to have come through.

Now, I don't know about that; I am not a scientist. But what I do know is that the Hebrew word *Adom* is the Hebrew word for "men," and what the Bible is saying is that God created men, not just Adam and Eve but people. And you already have the first creation story where God said, "Let us create them male and female," and God created them in God's image.

I realize this cuts across what all of us have believed for almost all of our religious lives. And in the theological world, it is the hottest button being touched today. I just read last week that two more professors have lost their jobs in prestigious seminaries because of their stand on Adam and Eve not being the couple who gave rise to all of humanity. I read last week that this is going to be the new Galileo. Do you know what I mean by that?

Sixteen hundred years ago, Galileo said the Earth revolves around the sun and the sun does not revolve around the Earth. The Catholic Church said, "Heretic," and put him in jail. It took the Roman Catholic Church until 1994 to apologize to him. Why did it take that long? Well, all the Roman Catholic leaders are men, and you know how long it takes us. The way to move through this is what I have been harping on all summer. When we do not take the Bible literally but take it interpretively and seriously, then these things are not problematic. When I come to Genesis and realize that when it is read in the Hebrew, it is poetry. So Genesis is poetry, and when poetry speaks to us, we do not make it literal.

I was out on my front porch and was feeling so weak and just helpless, and I looked at this oak tree, and this oak tree said to me, "You can be as deeply rooted as I am. You can be as strong as I am. You can drop acorns and produce little ones like I do." You think that tree said all that? Poetry speaks magnificently and marvelously, but it is poetry, and Genesis is poetry. It tells us that God created us. Not four thousand years ago. That is making it say something it does not say. God created humankind, and out of that creation He pulled Adam and Eve and said, "I created this beautiful story of where you come from." And we want to literalize it. And that is what gets us in trouble.

In God's eyes, all humankind is equal in creation. I realize that there are denominations among us who want to take Genesis's second creation and Eve's temptation and subsequent temptation of the man, and they want to make a booger out of Eve. That is not taking the scriptures sensibly. It is taking them literally and making them do and say things they were never meant to say.

II. God Is Impartial According to Ethnicity—Acts 10:34-35; Romans 10:12; Galatians 2:6

Secondly, in this creation of equality, God is not playing favorites ethnically either. You go back and look at the Genesis story, specifically in Genesis chapter 12 where God calls Abraham. And keep in mind I am not just now a heretic. I have been a heretic all my life. When I became a person of faith at age twenty-one and started reading the Bible like I had read every Zane Grey book (that means from the front to the back), I got to this twelfth chapter of Genesis, and God called Abraham. I remember just sitting up and saying, "Why him? Why not John or Sam? And why are you going to bless him, and why you going to curse him? If somebody curses him, you are going to curse them. If somebody blesses him, you are going to bless them. Why are you being prejudice? Why are you showing favoritism?"

Now I know what my Presbyterian brothers and sisters say. They say, "It is none of your business. God is sovereign, and God can do what God wants to do; you just need to shut up and go on." Well, I can't shut up, and I won't go on. But as I struggled with that, I looked at the text, and it is right there in the text. God said He would bless all these people and everything else for one reason. You know what that is? In order for you to be a blessing. God did not call out Israel and say, "There is something about you that is magnificently wonderful, and I am going to make you my people." No no no. God said, "I am calling you to be an instrument, a conduit, a pipe to the rest of the world through which my blessings can flow." And God blesses you, and God blesses me today for one reason and one reason only: not that we might horde those blessings but that we might pass them on. And if we are not passing them on, we are not getting them. Or we are not getting them like we could get them if we were not letting those blessings flow through us and onto someone else.

I think I mentioned this last week, but there is a crucial, crucial experience in the tenth chapter of Acts. If what happened in the tenth chapter of Acts had not happened, we would not be here today as a church. The church would not be in existence. Christianity would have died in that little far corner of the world as a Jewish sect, and it would not have been heard of. But on that rooftop Peter had a vision, and he saw this sheet come down and the Word of God saying, "Peter, kill and eat." And Peter said, "I don't eat that stuff. That is not kosher. That is non-Jewish stuff.

Jews do not eat crayfish and shrimp and lobsters. You got pigs on that sheet. No no no, we don't do that." And God said, "Peter, don't you dare call unclean what I have made clean." Three times he had that vision.

Then there was a knock at the door, and man at the door happened to be Gentile, which is a non-Jew. The Jews considered them Gentile dogs, did not associate with them, and did not eat with them. In fact, the Pharisees were called the "bruised and the bleeding." And do you know why they were called the bruised and the bleeding? Anytime they were walking down the street in Jerusalem and they saw a Gentile coming toward them, they took their cloaks, wrapped them over their heads so they would not be contaminated by this non-Jewish person, and with the cloaks over their heads, they would run into posts and walls and everything else and get all bloodied and bruised, and that is why they were called the bruised and the bleeding.

And the Gentile said to Peter, "While in prayer, we got a word from God that said you should come over and pray with us and told us where to find you." And Peter said, "It doesn't have anything to do with food. It has everything to do with people." And then Peter said, "I now understand God does not show favoritism." Had that not happened, folks, that little Jewish movement would not have opened its doors to the rest of the non-Jewish world, and we would not be here today. The church would not be in existence. And it comes out of God's deep sense of equality of all people.

III. God Is Impartial According to Gender—Galatians 3:26-29

God's equality goes beyond gender. I will deal with that next week fully. So, ladies, put on your best and come prepared. In the Galatians text it says, did you catch it, that there are no males or females. We are all equal. We are all equal in the sight of God.

IV. God Is Impartial According to Social Standing—Job 34:19; James 2:1-10

James tells us that God is not impartial to our social standing. I hope you will read that whole passage in the second chapter of James, verses 1-10. James says you have this party, you have this gathering, and this rich person comes in, and you say to him, "Let me get you a seat right up here in the front row where you can see good, and you can have the altar drippings." A poor guy comes in, and you put him back in the back room where we don't have any chairs left. You just stand. James says you are showing favoritism, and God abhors that because God does not show social favoritism.

I remember the first time I ever had to go to court. When I met with my lawyer before the court date, he said to me as he looked down at my Bass weejuns, "Do you have some black wing tips"? I said, "Yes, they are my funeral shoes." He said, "Wear them when you come to court." Then he said, "You got a black suit?" I said, "Yes, sir. That is my funeral suit." He said, "Wear it when you come to court." Then he said, "You got a red power tie?" I said, "Yes, sir." He said, "Wear it." I said, "Is all that *that* important?" He said, "Absolutely."

That is just what James is saying here, that our world looks on the outside. If you are dressed well enough, if you drive a good enough car, you are okay. But God says you are okay period. Where equality gets us in trouble is what C.S. Lewis explained it so well in his little book *Screwtape Letters*. Screwtape is a demon working up here on Earth. In this little book, he attacks equality. And for equality to work, according to C.S. Lewis—and keep in mind he is poking fun at it—he said a child who is smart and bright has to lower his or her work to the level of another child who is not so smart and bright so that there might be equality. You know we have done some of that. No more star player. Let's give the whole team a trophy. That is not equality. That is not what equality means. Equality means we are all the same in God's sight. We are all the same when it comes to dignity and to rights.

Are there people smarter than you are? Absolutely. Smarter than me? I hope so. Bigger, stronger, weaker, smarter—it's all just a rainbow, and that is the way it ought to be. And those who can do the finest ought to be pushed to do the finest. And those of us who can't, we do the best we can. I know what it means to lie on the canvas in a daze, looking at the other people's hands raised up. I know what that feels like. I know what losing feels like. But losing is good for us. Everyone can't have his or her hand up. Someone has to lose. That has nothing to do with equality.

CONCLUSION

I will tell you quickly what equality is. My church had a little trouble understanding this last year, and they were quizzing me about it. I had sat in the Kershaw prison in a little bitty chaplain's cubicle, looking into the face of a thirty-four-year-old, into the black eyes of a man who had killed, shot to death his estranged girlfriend, her mother, and her new lover. Part of my people could not understand how I could sit with that person and give pastoral care and pastoral psychotherapy to someone who had just taken out three images of God.

And I said it was simple. There seated in front of me was an image of God also. I didn't know how wounded he had been, I didn't know what he had been through to bring him to the point where he could do what he did, but what I deeply believed with every fiber of my being was that sitting there in front of me was an image of God, and I respected that person as an image of God. And when we can come to that place where that basic fundamental is an absolute acceptance, that no matter what his or her color, religion, or sexual preference, every person is created in the image of God, then we will respect them as such. Let us pray.

Lord Jesus, Lord of all, God our father, creator of all, we praise You for creating all of us in Your image with dignity, spirit, and soul. Remind us at our deepest level of being that we are all one. One spirit child of a spirit God. May it be so in Jesus's name. Amen.

THOUGHT PROVOKERS

I do not take literally the law that we should stone to death a bride if she proves not to be a virgin on her wedding night.

> If a man takes a wife and, after sleeping with her, dislikes her and slanders her and gives her a bad name, saying, "I married this woman, but when I approached her, I did not find proof of her virginity," then the young woman's father and mother shall bring to the town elders at the gate proof that she was a virgin. Her father will say to the elders, "I gave my daughter in marriage to this man, but he dislikes her. Now he has slandered her and said, 'I did not find your daughter to be a virgin.' But here is the proof of my daughter's virginity." Then her parents shall display the cloth before the elders of the town, and the elders shall take the man and punish him. They shall fine him a hundred shekels of silver and give them to the young woman's father, because this man has given an Israelite virgin a bad name. She shall continue to be his wife; he must not divorce her as long as he lives.

> If, however, the charge is true and no proof of the young woman's virginity can be found, she shall be brought to the door of her father's house and there the men of her town shall stone her to death. She has done an outrageous thing in Israel by being promiscuous while still in her father's house. You must purge the evil from among you. (Deut. 22:13-21 NIV)

CHAPTER 12

I Do Not Take Literally the Bible's Inequality of Women

SERMON SYLLABUS

Text: 1 Corinthians 11:2-10; 14:33-35; 1 Timothy 2:9-15; 1 Peter 3:1-6

CIT: Women were bound by the religious and social customs of that day.

Thesis: In Christ, women are free from the customs of biblical days.

Purpose:
- Major Objective: Ethical/Actional
- Specific Objective: Through the power of the Holy Spirit, I hope to lead each of us in experiencing the freedom of Christ.

Introduction

Outline:
   I. The Bible says: Women Are to Be Submissive—Ephesians 5:22; Colossians 3:18; 1 Peter 3:1
  II. The Bible says: Women Are to Be Silent—1 Corinthians 14:34; 1 Timothy 2:12; 3:11; 1 Peter 3:1
  III. The Bible says: Women Are to Be Saintly—1 Corinthians 11:6; 1 Timothy 2:9; 1 Peter 3:2-4

Conclusion

THE WORD OF THE LORD

1 Corinthians 11:2-10

> I praise you for remembering me in everything and for holding to the traditions just as I passed them on to you. But I want you to realize that the head of every man is Christ, and the head of the woman is man, and the head of Christ is God. Every man who prays or prophesies with his head covered dishonors his head. But every woman who prays or prophesies with her head uncovered dishonors her head—it is the same as having her head shaved. For if a woman does not cover her head, she might as well have her hair cut off; but if it is a disgrace for a woman to have her hair cut off or her head shaved, then she should cover her head.
>
> A man ought not to cover his head, since he is the image and glory of God; but woman is the glory of man. For man did not come from woman, but woman from man; neither was man created for woman, but woman for man. It is for this reason that a woman ought to have authority over her own head, because of the angels.

1 Corinthians 14:33-35

"For God is not a God of disorder but of peace—as in all the congregations of the Lord's people.

Women should remain silent in the churches. They are not allowed to speak, but must be in submission, as the law says. If they want to inquire about something, they should ask their own husbands at home; for it is disgraceful for a woman to speak in the church."

1 Timothy 2:9-15

> I also want the women to dress modestly, with decency and propriety, adorning themselves, not with elaborate hairstyles or gold or pearls or expensive clothes, but with good deeds, appropriate for women who profess to worship God.
>
> A woman should learn in quietness and full submission. I do not permit a woman to teach or to assume authority over a man;

she must be quiet. For Adam was formed first, then Eve. And Adam was not the one deceived; it was the woman who was deceived and became a sinner. But women will be saved through childbearing—if they continue in faith, love and holiness with propriety.

1 Peter 3:1-6

Wives, in the same way submit yourselves to your own husbands so that, if any of them do not believe the word, they may be won over without words by the behavior of their wives, when they see the purity and reverence of your lives. Your beauty should not come from outward adornment, such as elaborate hairstyles and the wearing of gold jewelry or fine clothes. Rather, it should be that of your inner self, the unfading beauty of a gentle and quiet spirit, which is of great worth in God's sight. For this is the way the holy women of the past who put their hope in God used to adorn themselves. They submitted themselves to their own husbands, like Sarah, who obeyed Abraham and called him her lord. You are her daughters if you do what is right and do not give way to fear.

INTRODUCTION

I heard a little choking going on in the congregation. I took a handwritten copy of the sermon syllabus to Toni, our office manager, and as I gave it to her to print, I said to her, "I am looking for that kind of woman." She looked down at the outline, and she looked back at me and said "Good luck on that here."

Here is a very clear classic example of what I have been trying to say all summer. Look at the central idea on the sermon syllabus. If you take these scriptures literally, then women are bound by religious custom and social morals of the biblical days. If you take these texts interpretively, you can say like I have in the thesis: in Christ, women are free from the religious customs and ritual morals of the biblical days.

Now these texts in this sermon are as current as today's newspaper. Brian York in Ohio asked Michelle Bachman, who is a biblical literalist, "If you are elected president, will you be submissive to your husband?"

And she answered, "Submissive means respect. Next question." I am sorry. Go to Webster. If we do not have some definitional regulations, we can't even communicate. There is nothing in Webster's definition of *submissive* about respect. Absolutely nothing, not so, not there. You will find words like *consent*; you will find words like *yielding control to authority*; you will find words like *humble*. But you will not find *respect*. Respect has nothing to do with being submissive.

Hoopo Tazo is the Greek word for submissive, and it is a military term. It comes from a Hebrew military term that means to "fall into formation." That is what the word *submissive* means. I will submit; I will fall into formation in relationship to your desires, your wants, and your instructions. That is what submissive means according to the Greeks and according to Webster. Now, I am not being political here. But if we vote and elect a woman who is a biblical literalist into the presidency of this country, we had better find out what her husband believes, because he is going to be running it. And we had better not leave him in the closet without coming out and saying what he believes and how he would run this country, because if she really believes what she says she believes, she will not be running it; he will. If you believe that a woman's place is to be submissive, you can't approach this any other way.

I. WOMEN ARE TO BE SUBMISSIVE—EPHESIANS 5:22; COLOSSIANS 3:18; 1 PETER 3:1

I don't know how many weddings I have attended where the male preacher will use Ephesians chapter 5 as his text. I didn't put that in here, but I could have used it too: "Wives submit yourselves to your husband." (Eph. 5:22) But I have never heard a male minister use verse 21 of chapter 5 that says, "Husbands, wives, submit yourselves unto each other as unto the Lord." Never have I heard that text at a wedding in all my years, and I submit that you haven't either. We always—no, they always—go to verse 22: "Wives submit yourselves to your husband in all things."

If you take this text literally and you employ it literally, you have a woman yielding to the authority of her husband. This word, *Hoopo Tazo*, is the same Greek word that is used in the slave text I used just a few weeks ago, which says, "Slaves submit yourselves to your master whether that master is a gentleman or not." It's the same word, and it means the same thing. Can't get away from it. If you take this text literally, that is what you have. Total submission of a woman in her home to her husband. But see, it goes outward from there. Listen to the rest of the text. The outline says the biblical picture of a woman is that she is submissive, and she is silent, and she is saintly. Isn't that a great picture, men? Wouldn't you just love it? Over and over again this text says let the women remain silent in churches; it is a disgrace for a woman to speak in the church.

II. WOMEN ARE TO BE SILENT—1 CORINTHIANS 14:34; 1 TIMOTHY 2:12; 3:11; 1 PETER 3:1

There are Southern Baptists here, and I love you, but your denomination about ten years ago—at least some of your denominations about ten years ago—decided to be serious about this text and quit allowing women to teach. What happened? How long did that last? One Sunday school semester because they didn't have any teachers.

What would happen at Liberty Hill if we pulled our women out of the church and said, "You must be silent"? There goes the choir; there goes the teachers for our children; there goes the teachers for our youth; there goes 90 percent of the participation in the adult Sunday school class that I teach. Ladies, no no no, sorry, you've got to remain silent. You can't ask a question. You can't venture your opinion. No no no, the Bible says no, can't do that. If you are concerned about something or you want to know something, keep your mouth shut, and go home ask your husband. Is that not what it says? Did I not just read that a minute ago? I did.

You know, we say we take the Bible literally, and we lie. And what I am saying is we need to quit saying that. We need to tell the truth. Most of us take the Bible interpretively. We read it, and we interpret it and try to apply it. We don't take it literally; we just like to throw that out there. We have political people who run around saying, "Yes, I take it literally." My perspective is that they are trying to build up a little respect from the people. They are losing their own respect because they don't do what they say they do. You just look at the many accounts we have gone through this summer and look at what would happen if you took this text literally and what would happen here in church if you took this text literally. The first thing we would have to do is pull every woman out of our churches, off our boards, off our commission, off our committees.

Let me present something else to you. Did you notice that the text that says, "I do not permit a woman to teach or to have authority over a man"? If a woman who is a biblical literalist wants to run for the president, the commander in chief of this nation, yet continues to say, "I take the scriptures literally," that is an oxymoron. Who will that female be teaching? As commander in chief, she would teach our military. You see, we don't think about this stuff and carry it through.

It doesn't make any difference if the women are silent anyway. I was in town several years ago in Columbia and happened to be on the street walking, and this car pulled up at the red light, and because of the commotion going on in the car, it caught my eye. This woman had slid up on the front of the seat and was looking right in the driver's face. They were hearing and speech impaired people apparently, and she was right in his face just going at it. Talking on her hands, I mean, just right in his face. She jumped out of the car and slammed the door and was looking in the window going (hand signs), and I was thinking, *You know, I used to think I would like to have a silent woman, but it don't make any difference.* I mean, ladies, you are going to get your point across; it doesn't make any difference if you use words or not. But the Bible says let the women be submissive, silent, and—I love this one—saintly.

III. Women Are to Be Saintly—1 Corinthians 11:6; 1 Timothy 2:9; 1 Peter 3:2-4

I don't know what picture you have when that word comes up, but the picture I have is a Pentecostal woman. God bless you, I love you too if you are here as a Pentecostal. I have had some wonderful Pentecostal friends. The women wear their dresses longer than my pants, and they have this big old bee hive hair up on their head and of course no makeup and no jewelry. That is the picture of a saintly woman. Not much of a sexual turn on or anything. But you know what the text says. Wives, be submissive. Your beauty should not come from outward adornment. Don't braid your hair. Don't wear any gold. Don't wear any jewelry or fine clothes. Instead work on your inner self, which is not a bad thing, the unfading beauty of a gentle, quiet spirit. Submissive, silent, saintly.

I have been doing marriage counseling for forty-five years. The healthiest marriages I see are marriages based on equality and mutuality.

The unhealthiest marriages I see, the most troubled marriages I see, the most dysfunctional marriages I see are marriages based on the "biblical pattern of a Christian home." I think we can take this text and understand it interpretively and struggle to apply what it says, but when you literalize it—I want a woman who is submissive, silent, and saintly—you are going to have a doormat, and there is no fun living with a doormat. A lot of this text is responsible—and I am going to get some criticism for this—for South Carolina being one of the leading states in the United States for domestic violence and spousal abuse and spousal death.

CONCLUSION

My client looked at me out of one eye. Her left eye was closed completely. She said to me, "My husband did this four nights ago." And then she said, "I went to my pastor, and he got his Bible, and he read this text to me: 'Wives in the same way be submissive to your husbands so that if any of them do not believe the Word, they may be won over without words by the behavior of their wives when they see the purity and the reverence of your life.'" And he said to her, "You must stay with him, and you must take his abuse, and you must live before him as a person of inner beauty and commitment to your God and your life, and the testimony of your life will be the witness that brings him to Christ."

I could wish. I could wish that she was here today to give you that testimony, but she is not; she is dead. She is dead by the same hands that blackened that eye, and he is in prison serving a thirty-year sentence, and there are three children who were separated and placed in relatives' homes. We cannot accept it any longer. We cannot any longer accept this kind of inequality of a human being. Paul, in all this text, never once mentioned the first creation story where male and female were created in God's image. Paul acts as if that is not part of his Bible. He was deeply, deeply biased. We do not have to take his bias literally. God gave us a spirit, and it dwells in us, and God gave us a mind, and when we see something as incongruent, inhumane, inhuman as the inequality of women, we need to stand up and say enough is enough.

Let us pray.

O Lord, thank You for this prized book I hold in my hand. It is one of the greatest books of faith our world has ever produced. Forgive us for misusing it and abusing it and having it in our hands as a tool to subjugate other people, especially our wives. Forgive us and help us to see a new day dawning, especially in our domestic-violence-ridden state. May it be so. In Jesus's name, amen.

THOUGHT PROVOKERS

I do not literally believe that a woman who has committed adultery should be killed. Neither did Jesus.

But Jesus went to the Mount of Olives.

At dawn he appeared again in the temple courts, where all the people gathered around him, and he sat down to teach them. The teachers of the law and the Pharisees brought in a woman caught in adultery. They made her stand before the group and said to Jesus, "Teacher, this woman was caught in the act of adultery. In the Law Moses commanded us to stone such women. Now what do you say?" They were using this question as a trap, in order to have a basis for accusing him.
But Jesus bent down and started to write on the ground with his finger. When they kept on questioning him, he straightened up and said to them, "Let any one of you who is without sin be the first to throw a stone at her." Again he stooped down and wrote on the ground.

At this, those who heard began to go away one at a time, the older ones first, until only Jesus was left, with the woman still standing there. Jesus straightened up and asked her, "Woman, where are they? Has no one condemned you?"

"No one, sir," she said.

"Then neither do I condemn you," Jesus declared. "Go now and leave your life of sin." (John 8:1-11 NIV)

CHAPTER 13

I TAKE SERIOUSLY THE BIBLE'S IDENTITY OF JESUS

SERMON SYLLABUS

Text: Matthew 16:13-17; 26:62-64; Luke 2:11

CIT: The Bible claimed that Jesus was the promised Messiah, the Son of God.

Thesis: Jesus is our Savior and Lord.

Purpose:
- Major Objective: Doctrinal
- Specific Objective: Through the power of the Holy Spirit, I hope to lead each of us in affirming Jesus as Lord and Savior.

Introduction

Outline:
I. The Angels Declared Who Jesus Was—Luke 2:11
II. God Declared Who He Was—Mark 1:9-11
III. Jesus Declared Who He Was—Matthew 26:62-64; John 4:25-26; 3:1
IV. The Disciples Declared Who Jesus Was—Matthew 16:1-17; John 1:40-41
V. Paul Declared Who Jesus Was—Acts 9:21-22
VI. I Declare Who Jesus Is!

Conclusion

The Word of the Lord

Matthew 16:13-17

When Jesus came to the region of Caesarea Philippi, he asked his disciples, "Who do people say the Son of Man is?"

They replied, "Some say John the Baptist; others say Elijah; and still others, Jeremiah or one of the prophets."

"But what about you?" he asked. "Who do you say I am?"

Simon Peter answered, "You are the Messiah, the Son of the living God."

Jesus replied, "Blessed are you, Simon son of Jonah, for this was not revealed to you by flesh and blood, but by my Father in heaven.

Matthew 26:62-64

Then the high priest stood up and said to Jesus, "Are you not going to answer? What is this testimony that these men are bringing against you?" But Jesus remained silent.

The high priest said to him, "I charge you under oath by the living God: Tell us if you are the Messiah, the Son of God."

"You have said so," Jesus replied. "But I say to all of you: From now on you will see the Son of Man sitting at the right hand of the Mighty One and coming on the clouds of heaven."

Luke 2:11

"Today in the town of David a Savior has been born to you; he is the Messiah, the Lord."

INTRODUCTION

Who is this Jesus that we sang about? Have you seen *Talladega Nights*, a movie on NASCAR racing featuring a fictitious character named Ricky Bobby, played by Will Ferrell. If I can't take at least one line or one scene away from a movie and have it stay with me, I feel like the movie was a failure. This is one of the things I took away from *Talladega Nights*.

They are at Domino's or someplace having a meal, and Ricky Bobby gets up to say grace. His wife, Carly; his buddy, Cal; her father; and some others, along with one of their children are there, and he starts off his grace, "Dear Lord baby Jesus," and he thanks little baby Jesus for his red hot wife, and he goes on. Finally, Carly interrupts him and says, "Honey, you don't have to pray to baby Jesus. You can pray to adult Jesus." And he says, "I am saying grace. You pray to adult Jesus or teenage Jesus or bearded Jesus or whomever you want to pray to. I like the Christmas story. I like to pray to baby Jesus." And he continued, "Little six pound eight ounce baby Jesus in that little cradle, omnipotent even then." And he thanks Him for all of his NASCAR winnings and all of this other stuff. Who is this Jesus that we all talk about and pray to?

In 1972, Larry Norman wrote a song titled "The Outlaw." I am not going to sing it. I got enough criticism just a few weeks ago. One person had the nerve to call me and say, "Do not give up your day job." I have strong feelings, but boy they were hurt, I mean to tell you. But here is Larry Norman's song titled "The Outlaw":

> Some say he was an outlaw, that he roamed across the land,
> With a band of unschooled ruffians and few old fishermen,
> No one knew just where he came from, or exactly what he'd done,
> But they said it must be something bad that kept him on the run.
>
> Some say he was a poet, that he'd stand upon the hill
> That his voice could calm an angry crowd and make the waves stand still,
> That he spoke in many parables that few could understand,
> But the people sat for hours just to listen to this man.

Some say he was a sorcerer, a man of mystery,
He could walk upon the water, he could make a blind man see,
That he conjured wine at weddings and did tricks with fish and bread,
That he talked of being born again and raised people from the dead.

Some say a politician who spoke of being free,
He was followed by the masses on the shores of Galilee,
He spoke out against corruption and he bowed to no decree,
And they feared his strength and power so they nailed him to a tree.

Some say he was the Son of God, a man above all men,
That he came to be a servant and to set us free from sin,
And that's who I believe he is cause that's what I believe,
And I think we should get ready cause it's time for us to leave.[1]

I. THE ANGELS DECLARED WHO JESUS WAS—LUKE 2:11

"The Outlaw." Who is this Jesus? Well, the angels declared to the shepherds out in the field—this is the favorite story in *Talladega Nights*. The angels said to the shepherds, "Today in the city of David a Savior who is Christ the Lord has been born." So there was an announcement, a declaration from the heralds of the sky that this Jesus who hsad just been born was a Savior, Son of God, the Messiah, the Promised One. So our first glimpse of Jesus in this beautiful Christmas story is the declaration that Jesus is the Savior of the world, the promised Messiah, the Son of God. So it was first declared by the angels. Then as John the Baptist came forward to baptize Jesus at about age thirty, as He came up out of the water, God made a declaration. God declared, "This is my beloved son in whom I am well pleased."

II. GOD DECLARED WHO HE WAS—MARK 1:9-11

I think as I deal with men in my therapy practice that if they have never heard that declaration from their earthly fathers, there is a deep vacuum, a hole, a psychic hole that longs to be filled by that declaration from their male parents: "My beloved son in whom I am well pleased." I never received that, having lost my father when I was age four, but I will come back to that later. How important this need is, and God said on the shores of Galilee as Jesus came up out of the water, "This is my beloved son in whom I am well pleased." So the angels declared that this Jesus was the Savior, the Son of God, the promised Jewish Messiah, and now we have a voice from the heavens declaring, "Jesus is my beloved son." Not only did the angels and God himself declare it, but Jesus declared it.

III. Jesus Declared Who He Was—Matthew 26:62-64; John 4:25-26; 3:1

Jesus was always little bit hedgy about that. If you read the scriptures carefully, He just didn't walk around with a placard that said, *Hello, my name is Jesus. I am the Savior of the world the Son of God.* He didn't go by a T-shirt shop and have it put on the front and the back of a T-shirt: *Follow me. I am Jesus, the Son of God.* He was just a bit humble about that and did not broadcast it much. In fact, at times when someone would say it, He would say to them, "*Shhh,* don't spread that around. It is not just the right time for that to be spread around, too popular." But at His trial, the chief priest said to Him, "Do not remain silent any longer about these accusations. In God's name, tell us the truth." And as the high priest said, "Are you the son of God? Are you Christ?" You notice what Jesus said in the text? "It is as you say." So not only do we have this declaration from the angels, we have this declaration from creator God, God's self, and we have this declaration from Jesus. Jesus declares, "Yes, what they are saying about me is the truth."

IV. The Disciples Declared Who Jesus Was—Matthew 16:1-17; John 1:40-41

It is also declared by His disciples. Very early in the beginning, as He was walking on the shores of Galilee, He had been doing some preaching, and He had attracted some attention, and these fishermen left their nets and started following him. Andrew, one of the first ones, realized in his spirit who this was, and he ran to get his stronger brother, Peter, the outspoken (hoof-in-mouth Peter). Andrew said to Peter, "Come and see who I just met. It is Jesus the Christ, the promised Messiah." And from there the little band of twelve began to form. Later on in their ministry, Jesus just said to them pointedly, "Who do people say I am?"

See how that question keeps coming up? And some of them said, "Well, you know, there is talk about John the Baptist resurrecting." You know, that is where we get the Elvis resurrection from, you remember? "They say John the Baptist has resurrected, and you are the resurrection. Others say that you are the second Elijah. Others say Jeremiah, one of the prophets."

And Jesus brought it real personal like all of us must be confronted at some point and time in our lives: "Who do you say that I am? What about you? No longer what do they say. What do you say?" And Peter said, "You are Christ the Son of the living God." What a confession. And Jesus said to Peter, "You did not come to that through your own realization. You didn't come to that through your own analyzing what I have said and what I have done. You came to that conclusion through the revelation of the Holy Spirit."

And I think that is how we all have to come to that conclusion. And that is why years ago I quit trying to convince people by argument because I realized if I convinced them who Jesus was by argument, they were simply at the mercy of the next most clever argument. So I just quit doing that. I also realized it was not in my job description. My job description was simply to declare. If anybody does any convincing, that is the Holy Spirit's job description, not mine. I remember the day I had that revelation. Such freedom. You know, I have sung fifteen verses of "Just as I Am," to finally get to the point of saying: "If you love your mama, come on down front." I got to have some statistics to turn in Monday morning. That is an awful way to live. That is not my responsibility. That is the Holy Spirit's. It is just mine to declare. So here we have the disciples declaring clearly that Jesus is the Son of God.

V. PAUL DECLARED WHO JESUS WAS—ACTS 9:21-22

And then along came Paul, persecutor of the church and stoner of Steven, going around locking people up and confiscating property of Christians.

He did such a good job in Jerusalem that they gave him papers to go to Damascus, and on the road to Damascus, he was struck down by a light, and the voice said, "Paul, why are you persecuting me?" And Paul said, "I don't know who you are." And He told him who He was. And immediately the scriptures say Paul went to Damascus and fervently declared that this Jesus, whom he had been persecuting, was the Son of God, the Christ, the promised Messiah. So fervently he preached that they attempted to kill him. And you know that little childhood story you learned in Bible School? They let him down in this basket over the wall, and he got away. So Jesus, Son of God, the promised Messiah, Savior of our world, was declared by all of these men. Now, if you missed all of that, so you won't totally crucify me next Sunday, listen to my declaration.

VI. I DECLARE WHO JESUS IS!

Jesus is my Lord and my Savior. When I was unforgiven, Jesus came to me as God's expression of grace. When I was unforgivable, Jesus came to me as God's expression of forgiveness. When I was unlovely, and yeah even unlovable, God in Christ Jesus came and loved me. He has been and is the model of love for my life that I have never lived up to and would never dare compare myself to, but He has been my goal and my idol and my model to live after. That is for me.

I have Islamic friends, especially the Sufies, who love more deeply than I could ever love and who are more compassionate to humankind than I could ever be. I have an Imam friend, and that means he is a minister in the Islamic faith, who is totally and absolutely devoted to the most unloving, unlovable people in our world—our prisoners. They are incarcerated, and day in and day out, he demonstrates a love of God and the compassion of God to these people. I have a dear friend who is a Jewish chaplain in St. Louis, Missouri, who I experience as so much more compassionate than me. So much more deeply committed to his call than me. I have Buddhist brothers and sisters who love God without exception as much or more than I do. But that is not my way. The way I have found is Jesus the Christ, who came to me as a twenty-one-year-old psychically lost and depressed, emotionally wounded, socially marred, parentally unfit, and He came to me with the love of God and the forgiveness of God.

CONCLUSION

Blake Greenway wrote a song titled "If He Was Just a Man," and he says the following in this song:

> I have heard his name most all of my life,
> they tell me he once healed a blind man's eyes,
> they tell me he walked on the sea
> they tell me that he gave his own life for me
> but if I really told the truth, I would say sometimes
> I've doubted just like you.
> But there is one thing I go back to,
> There is one question I would like to ask you
> If he is just a man, there is one thing I cannot understand
> How could he change my life so if he was just a man.[2]

My life was touched in such a way that I have never been able to doubt that Jesus is the Christ, my Savior, my way to forgiveness and salvation. Who is Jesus to you? Jesus's question to the disciples, "Who do you say that I am?" May that question linger with you. Who do you say that He is?

Let us pray. Lord Jesus, You baffled people in Your day, and in the seventh chapter of John, some were saying You were a lunatic; others were saying You were a good man; others were saying You were a teacher; and a few cried out that You were the Son of God. Help us in these moments to look deeply within ourselves and hear that question rumble through the hallways of our minds and into the depths of our souls and spirits: who do I say that You are? May that question rest easy upon our hearts because we know who You are, or may it rest heavily upon our hearts because we are undecided, but let it rest upon us. In Jesus's name, amen.

NOTES

1. Martin Thielen, *What's the Least I can Believe and Still be a Christian?* (Louisville: Westminster Press, 2011), 69.
2. Ibid., 72.

THOUGHT PROVOKERS

I do not take the virgin birth of Jesus literally.

Belief in the virgin birth may have been an honest mistake by the authors of the Gospels of Matthew and Luke.

Most theologians and historians who are not conservative Christians believe that the author of the Gospel of Matthew (or someone who supplied the writer with source material) scanned an unknown ancient Greek translation of the Hebrew scriptures. He found what he believed to be a reference to Jesus's birth. It was in Isaiah 7:14. This has since become a famous passage; it is often recited at Christmastime. He copied it into Matthew (1:23) to show that prophecies in the Hebrew Testament were fulfilled in Jesus's life.

As it happens, the Greek translators made a mistake. When they were translating the Hebrew writings into the Greek Septuagint and similar translations, they converted the Hebrew word *almah* into the Greek equivalent of our English word for virgin. *Almah* appears nine other times in the Hebrew scriptures; in each case it means "young woman." When the Hebrew scriptures referred to a virgin (and they do more than fifty times) they always used the Hebrew word *betulah*. So it appears certain that Isaiah referred to a young woman becoming pregnant—a relatively ordinary event.

Some English translators are accurate to the original Hebrew:

- Revised English Bible: ". . . a young woman is with child . . ."
- Revised Standard Version: ". . . a young woman shall conceive . . ."
- James Moffatt Translation: ". . . a young woman with child . . ."
- New Revised Standard Version: ". . . the young woman is with child . . ."

CHAPTER 14

I Do Not Take Literally the Bible's Virgin Birth of Jesus

Sermon Syllabus

Text: Isaiah 7:14; Matthew 1:18-25; Luke 1:26-38

CIT: The virgin birth of Jesus came from two Gospels eighty to eight-five years after His historical birth.

Thesis: The virgin birth of Jesus is not needed for Jesus to be our Savior and Lord.

Purpose:
- Major Objective: Doctrinal
- Specific Objective: Through the power of the Holy Spirit, I hope to lead each of us in affirming Jesus as Lord and Savior.

Introduction

Outline:
    I.   The Old Testament Did Not Prophesize that Jesus Would Be Born of a Virgin—Isaiah 7:14
    II. Paul Did Not Mention Jesus Being Born of a Virgin—Galatians 4:4; Romans 1:3
    III. Mark Did Not Mention Jesus Being Born of a Virgin—Mark 1:9-11
    IV. John Did Not Mention Jesus Being Born of a Virgin—John 1:1-5, 14, 45
    V.   Many Other Religious Traditions Have Virgin-Born Leaders
    VI. How Jesus Does Become Savior and Lord—Romans 1:2-4

Conclusion

THE WORD OF THE LORD

Isaiah 7:14
"Therefore the Lord himself will give you a sign: The virgin will conceive and give birth to a son, and will call him Immanuel."

Matthew 1:18-25
>This is how the birth of Jesus the Messiah came about: His mother Mary was pledged to be married to Joseph, but before they came together, she was found to be pregnant through the Holy Spirit. Because Joseph her husband was faithful to the law, and yet did not want to expose her to public disgrace, he had in mind to divorce her quietly.

>But after he had considered this, an angel of the Lord appeared to him in a dream and said, "Joseph, son of David, do not be afraid to take Mary home as your wife, because what is conceived in her is from the Holy Spirit. She will give birth to a son, and you are to give him the name Jesus, because he will save his people from their sins."

>All this took place to fulfill what the Lord had said through the prophet: "The virgin will conceive and give birth to a son, and they will call him Immanuel" (which means "God with us").

>When Joseph woke up, he did what the angel of the Lord had commanded him and took Mary home as his wife. But he did not consummate their marriage until she gave birth to a son. And he gave him the name Jesus.

Luke 1:26-38
>In the sixth month of Elizabeth's pregnancy, God sent the angel Gabriel to Nazareth, a town in Galilee, to a virgin pledged to be married to a man named Joseph, a descendant of David. The virgin's name was Mary. The angel went to her and said, "Greetings, you who are highly favored! The Lord is with you."

Mary was greatly troubled at his words and wondered what kind of greeting this might be. But the angel said to her, "Do not be afraid, Mary; you have found favor with God. You will conceive and give birth to a son, and you are to call him Jesus. He will be great and will be called the Son of the Most High. The Lord God will give him the throne of his father David, and he will reign over Jacob's descendants forever; his kingdom will never end."

"How will this be," Mary asked the angel, "since I am a virgin?"

The angel answered, "The Holy Spirit will come on you, and the power of the Most High will overshadow you. So the holy one to be born will be called the Son of God. Even Elizabeth your relative is going to have a child in her old age, and she who was said to be unable to conceive is in her sixth month. For no word from God will ever fail."

"I am the Lord's servant," Mary answered. "May your word to me be fulfilled." Then the angel left her.

INTRODUCTION

Let us begin with something we all can agree upon. So in the very beginning, let us find total agreement in this very diverse crowd. And that total agreement is this: I do not know what kind of condition Mary was in when Jesus was born. I do not know if she was a virgin. I do not know if she was not a virgin. I have no way of personally knowing any of that. Now, can you agree to that? You do not know that Mary was a virgin. You have no way of knowing experientially whether Mary was a virgin or not. So this morning can we agree that we are talking about something we cannot know. Experientially, empirically, can we agree to that? It is by faith that we come to believe this. It is by faith that we believe this story. So we are talking in the faith realm and not in the fact realm because none of us can know.

In my research, I was surprised to find that according to the latest Gallup polls, 80 percent of Americans believe in the virgin birth of Jesus Christ. That astonished me. For you see, that percentage is higher than the same Gallup polls shows spiritual belief in America. Well, let me rephrase that: spiritual involvement or religious involvement. The total percentage of all religious affiliations in America today, the polls say, is 67 percent. Sixty-seven percent of Americans belong to some form of religion institutionally. Eighty percent is higher than that. I was a bit astonished. And it made me feel bad. Most people believe something I do not believe, at least 80 percent.

My struggle with the virgin birth began in the very beginning of my faith. I was twenty-one, came down with the mumps, did not have a background in the church, was not raised in the church, had not read the Bible stories, and did not know the scripture. My mother quoted scripture and Shakespeare about the same way. I came to faith as a twenty-one-year-old while at home with the mumps. It was the first time I had been quiet in my life. The only books I had ever read were Zane Grey books, and I read them from front to back, so I started reading the Bible from front to back, and I couldn't make head or tails out of anything I was reading. "So and so begat so and so." I didn't even know what *begat* meant; so I finally got over into the book of Job, and I couldn't understand it, and then I went to the book of Psalms, and it didn't make any sense either. And then I went on to what they call the New Testament, and I read a little bit of St. Matthew, and all he started off with was "so and so begat so and so," and I went to St. Luke, and I wondered why these two men had the same first names. And then lo and behold, I found that Mark and John also had the same first names too. So I thought, *Well, they must be two common names*, but I settled in the book of John, and John made sense to me.

Out of that book the Spirit of God walked into my life at age twenty-one, and I have never been the same. My values changed, my behavior changed, my attitude changed, my life changed. I was baptized in my wife's Baptist church. I joined the Sunday school class. Three weeks after that, one of the couples in the class wanted us to go with them to a revival in downtown Spartanburg in a big meeting with a worldwide known evangelist of whom I had never heard, of course. So we went with this couple.

We had only been there a little while when this minister said, "If you do not believe the virgin birth, you are not a Christian." Well, I didn't believe it because John doesn't say anything about it. So I got up, and I told them I would meet them outside. I left, and I went outside and waited. I was not going to listen to that because I knew in my heart that God had touched me; my life had radically changed in just a matter of a few weeks. I had at least enough internal authority to say I didn't care how many little letters someone had behind his or her name and how many *reverends* someone had in front of his or her name; that was not compatible with my experience. I believed I was a Christian, and I did not believe in the virgin birth. I had never heard of it. So I got up and left.

Well, later I read Matthew and Luke, and they told of the virgin birth. I said okay. I just hadn't got that far yet. So I struggled with it, and I have struggled with it much of my ministry, but the struggle for me is over. I am clear, very clear in my mind about what I believe. Very clear in my heart about what I believe. I am a Christian, and I do not literally believe Jesus was born of a virgin. There is nothing about the salvation experience that says you have to believe in the virgin birth of Jesus to be a Christian. That is manmade, human imposed, and not true. I was and I am today a Christian. I may be like that fellow who confronted me at the beginning of the series when he read that I didn't believe in a literal burning hell. He looked at me in the eye and said, "You will find out." Well, maybe that is true. Maybe I will find out one day that I am not what I thought I was for all these years, but that is okay. The journey has been fantastic.

I. The Old Testament Did Not Prophesize that Jesus Would Be Born of a Virgin—Isaiah 7:14

I have trouble with the virgin birth for a number of reasons. One is that the Old Testament passage in Isaiah that the birth stories are based upon has its problems. The Hebrew word is *almah* in Isaiah 7:14. *Almah* is the Hebrew word for "young woman." The text is saying a young woman will bear a child. If you notice, I have put several things in your bulletin. I hope you will carry it home and look at a little closer. *Betulah* is the Hebrew word for "virgin." It is never translated in any other way the more than fifty times it appears in the Hebrew Bible.

Almah is in that verse, and it is translated to mean "virgin." *Virgin* is not the word in Isaiah 7:14. When they translated the Hebrew into Greek, which is called the Septuagint, that was the first translation ever of the Old Testament Hebrew into New Testament Greek, and that is what Jesus read. We have no indication that Jesus read Hebrew. He did speak Aramaic. He was fluent in Aramaic; that was his native language. He was also fluent in Greek. But we have no indication he ever spoke or read Hebrew. But His Bible at that time was the Septuagint, a Greek translation of the Old Testament Hebrew. And it was through some of those translations that in some Greek manuscripts the word *Parthonos*, which is the Greek word for "virgin," begins to show up. So the King James Bible, which translated the Old Testament from the Septuagint and not from the Hebrew, translated Isaiah 7:14 to read "virgin." Matthew and Luke picked up that translation and created a story around the virgin birth.

II. PAUL DID NOT MENTION JESUS BEING BORN OF A VIRGIN—GALATIANS 4:4; ROMANS 1:3

Paul never mentions the virgin birth. The closest Paul gets to it is in Galatians 4:4 when he speaks of Jesus and says that Jesus was born of a woman under the law. If Paul knew about the virgin birth and if he believed the virgin birth, why didn't he write about it? Why didn't he say something about it? Paul's writings are the earliest writings we have giving a testimony to Jesus. Between AD 50-65 is when Paul composed the earliest writings. Now, I know there are people who believe in the virgin birth simply because the book of Matthew is first in the New Testament. Therefore, they think Matthew was written first. Not so. Matthew and Luke were not written until AD 80-85. Paul's letters were written from AD 50-60, and Paul never mentions it. Paul mentions Jesus being born of human seed in the first chapter of Romans. I will refer to that later. Paul also mentions Jesus was born of a woman. He never mentions anything about a virgin birth.

III. MARK DID NOT MENTION JESUS BEING BORN OF A VIRGIN—MARK 1:9-11

Mark's Gospel is the first Gospel written. Mark does not say anything about a virgin birth. Mark picks up Jesus as an adult and tells the story of Jesus as an adult, beginning with John's baptism. Mark either did not know of a virgin birth, or if he had heard about it, he didn't believe it. Had it been important, he would have written about it. Mark does not have anything to say about the virgin birth.

IV. John Did Not Mention Jesus Being Born of a Virgin—John 1:1-5, 14, 45

John, the last Gospel to be written, was written between AD 90-105. John had to have known about the virgin birth. Stories in Matthew and Luke existed. He could not have been exposed to the Christian community without knowing it. Why did John not say something about the virgin birth? John said nothing about the virgin birth! In the first chapter of John, John talked about Jesus as being the son of Joseph. Twice in the Gospel of John, John talked about Jesus being the son of Joseph. Now what John did was make Jesus pre-existent. John made Jesus in heaven with God, pre-existing the virgin birth. But it seems to me that if John thought the virgin birth was important, especially important to our salvation, as some people want to insist, he would have said something about it. John says nothing about the virgin birth.

Okay, if Paul, the earliest writer, said nothing, and Mark, the first Gospel writer, said nothing, and John, the last Gospel writer, said nothing, why was it then that Matthew and Luke, who wrote their Gospels in about AD 80-85, mention it? Well, here is my belief, the belief according to Gene Rollins, and you don't have to agree with me. You know I don't care whether you agree with me or not. That is not important. I hope you understand it. I hope you understand where I am coming from, but you don't have to go there with me. You really don't, and we can still be friends.

I was talking to one of my grandsons this week. We talked seriously for a little over an hour about theology, and he said to me at the conclusion of the conversation, "Papa, I love you, you know I do." And I said, "Absolutely." But he said, "You are a complicated man." And I said to him, "Son, you have summed up the last hour of conversation with that statement. And that is what we are to be."

We are to love each other in all of our complications, in all of our different perceptions, in all of our ways of thinking and believing. You are a created child of God, and I love you. I don't care whether you agree with me or not. I said, "Son, you have captured it. Nothing else matters."

V. Many Other Religious Traditions Have Virgin-Born Leaders

Why then did Matthew and Luke do what they did? Well, let me touch on other religions first. And so I don't have to spend all that time going over them, here is a list of them. At least a list of the ones I know of.

Buddha, according to their religious tradition, was virgin born. Zoroaster was virgin born. You can go look at all the other founders of religious movements, and they too were virgin born. In Jesus's day, Mars the god of war produced twins, Romulus and Remus. A god impregnating a virgin produced these twin sons. These twin sons, Romulus and Remus, became founders of the Roman Empire that was in control of and occupied Israel during the entire life of Jesus. These men were virgin born. That was the story. Every Roman emperor from them, Ceasar Augustus, King Herrod—all of them—proclaimed virgin birth. All of them. And that is why they all required that they be addressed as Lord Ceasar, Lord Herrod, etc. You would lose your head if you didn't. So Jesus was there in the context of all these religious rulers who were virgin born and all of these political rulers and empire leaders who were virgin born, and he was a peasant from Nazareth. In many other religious traditions of the world, the concept of a virgin birth to explain the divine origin or heroic figures was commonplace. Check these out on your own:[1]

1. Gautama Buddha, the ninth avatar of India, was said to have been born of the virgin Maya about 600 BCE. The Holy Ghost was also portrayed as descending upon her.
2. Horus, a god of Egypt, was born of the virgin Isis, it was said, around 1550 BCE. Horus also received gifts from three kings in his infancy.
3. Attis was born of a virgin mother named Nama in Phrygia before 200 BCE.
4. Quirrnus, a Roman savior, was born of a virgin in the sixth century BCE. His death, it was said, was accompanied by universal darkness.
5. Indra was born of a virgin in Tibet in the eighth century BCE. He also was said to have ascended into heaven.

6. Adonsi, a Babylonian deity, was said to have been born of a virgin mother named Ishtar, who was later to be hailed as queen of heaven.
7. Mithra, a Persian deity, was also said to have been born of a virgin around 600 BCE.
8. Zoroaster likewise made his earthy appearance courtesy of a virgin mother.
9. Krishna, the eighth avatar of the Hindu pantheon, was born of the virgin Devaki around 1200 BCE.

Do you get the picture? How is a peasant from Nazareth going to establish an empire with all these virgin-born, god-sired people around? Well, we have a verse in the Old Testament, and that verse means that Jesus was born of a virgin. Isaiah 7:14 was written 730 years before Jesus's birth. King Ahaz, who had two warring kings breathing down his neck, went to Isaiah for some help, and Isaiah says to him, "A virgin will bear a son 730 years in the future. Aren't you happy?" Can't you see Ahaz saying, "Hello! I don't care about 730 years from now. I want to know what is going to happen today, tomorrow with these warring kings breathing down my neck." So how is it that a birth 730 years from now was going to help Ahaz in his situation? How? It doesn't make sense, but nothing is impossible with God. It doesn't have to make sense. We just have to believe it.

In the context of all these religious leaders and all these political leaders being virgin born, then Jesus Himself was virgin born, according to the story. And then from those stories, the Roman Catholic Church—and I know we have Roman sisters and brothers here, and I am not picking on you; I pick on the Presbyterians too—Rome just went to seed over Mary. When the pope speaks "ex catedra," it is infallible; it becomes law.

And the pope said that Mary, his first pronouncement, was a perpetual virgin, meaning she had Jesus, and then all his brothers and sisters had to be born the same kind of miraculous way, and she also maintained her virginity throughout her life. Jesus had at least three brothers and some sisters; we don't know how many.

And then the second thing the pope produced was that Mary was a postpartum virgin, meaning that before and after Jesus's birth her hymen was never broken. So before Jesus and after Jesus and through all the other births, Mary's hymen was never broken. Postpartum—that was a declaration by the pope. The third thing he said was that Mary herself was immaculately conceived. Do you know why they are going there? Makes sense. If sinfulness is passed on from mother to child, if we are born in sin, as some believe, if all of us have the sin of Adam, then how can Jesus be sinless if his mother passes this stain on to him? Well, he was virgin born. But we still have a problem with her, so the Catholic Church says, well, she was virgin born also.

So we have two generations of virgin births, and then finally the last pronouncement in 1956 from the Roman Catholic Church said that Mary was assumed into heaven bodily; she did not die. I don't believe any of that, any of it. I don't take any of it literally. Preacher, you have a problem then. If Jesus is your Savior as you proclaimed last week so loudly, how then is He your Savior if He was not virgin born? How can He be sinless? Well you see, I don't take literally that fall stuff. That is a poem. I don't take literally that we are born in sin. I don't take that literally.

And when I present your babies to our congregation, I do not say to the congregation, "Oh, look at this sweet little sinful thing, born in sin, this precious little thing I hold in my hand is totally depraved, absolutely sinful to the core." The Catholic Church believes that. If this little baby dies before it is baptized, it will go to hell. The Roman Catholic Church baptizes for original sin. In baptism, this original sin is washed away. But if the child is not baptized, it is doomed to hell. This is a precious innocent child I have in my hands who is dialectical, and the word *dialectical* means "intension." This child is in the image of God, but this child is a human creature, and this tension between this human creature and this Spirit of God is going to be in tension all of this child's life and all of its adult life. We are not created good or bad. We are created dialectical. We are God's children, God's spirit children, but we are human. Which one is going to have control of your life? That is the tension. How is it then that Jesus becomes our Savior?

VI. How Jesus Does Become Savior and Lord?—Romans 1:2-4

Well, Paul says it. Let me read it for you. Please listen carefully. In first chapter of Romans, Paul said it in verse 3. I just cried when I went back to this a few weeks ago. Listen: "Regarding his son who as to his human nature was a descendent of David and who through the spirit of holiness was declared with power to be the son of God by his resurrection from the dead Jesus Christ our Lord."

From my understanding, Paul just told us how Jesus became the Son of God. Did you get it? Through holiness! Have we ever had anyone who was as absolutely committed to the obedience of God and to the holiness of God as was Jesus? No! Jesus becomes my Savior through his obedience and holiness, not through some passage through a virgin's womb. The scripture tells us that Jesus was tempted in every way that we are (that is why I believe He was married), and yet He was without sin. He was without sin. How could He be so deeply committed? Because He was virgin born? If that is the case, I can't be that committed because I can't go back in the womb like Nicademus asked Jesus about and come out again.

CONCLUSION

My choice then is to struggle to be as obedient and struggle to be as holy and struggle to be as righteous as He was because He is my example; He is my mentor; He is my hero; He is who I am living after. I can go with that. But if I have to be virgin born, it is over with. I have no chance. Are you with me? Jesus became God's Son through His obedience, His holiness, His devotion, His commitment, and His absolute reliance upon the will, guidance, and leadership of His Holy Father. Therein is my Savior. Let us pray.

Lord Jesus, help us at this moment to feel agreement with each other in that we do not know. We simply do not know. We were not midwifing. And if we had been midwifing, I don't think we could have known. So, Lord, we don't know. We live by faith, and some of our faith differs from others' faith. Help us to love in the context of those differences. Help us to love in the context of those different commitments and ways of loving and serving You. And help us all as we struggle to have a faith that is pragmatic, meaningful, relevant, and life giving. May it be so in Jesus's name. Amen.

NOTES

1. John Shelby Spong, *Born of a Woman* (New York: Harper Collins Publishers, 1992), 56

THOUGHT PROVOKERS

I do not take literally the law that a person should be put to death if he or she works on the Sabbath (Sunday).

> Then the LORD said to Moses, "Say to the Israelites, 'You must observe my Sabbaths. This will be a sign between me and you for the generations to come, so you may know that I am the LORD, who made you holy.
>
> "'Observe the Sabbath, because it is holy to you. Anyone who desecrates it is to be put to death; those who do any work on that day must be cut off from their people. For six days work is to be done, but the seventh day is a day of Sabbath rest, holy to the LORD. Whoever does any work on the Sabbath day is to be put to death. The Israelites are to observe the Sabbath, celebrating it for the generations to come as a lasting covenant. It will be a sign between me and the Israelites forever, for in six days the LORD made the heavens and the earth, and on the seventh day he rested and was refreshed.'"
>
> When the LORD finished speaking to Moses on Mount Sinai, he gave him the two tablets of the covenant law, the tablets of stone inscribed by the finger of God. (Exod. 31:12-18 NIV)
>
> While the Israelites were in the wilderness, a man was found gathering wood on the Sabbath day. Those who found him gathering wood brought him to Moses and Aaron and the whole assembly, and they kept him in custody, because it was not clear what should be done to him.
>
> Then the LORD said to Moses, "The man must die. The whole assembly must stone him outside the camp." So the assembly took him outside the camp and stoned him to death, as the LORD commanded Moses. (Num. 15:32-36 NIV)

CHAPTER 15

I TAKE SERIOUSLY THE BIBLE'S AFFIRMATION OF GOD'S JUDGMENT

SERMON SYLLABUS

Text: Psalm 62:11-12; Matthew 16:27; 2 Corinthians 5:10; Revelation 20:11-15

CIT: A major theme in the Bible was God's final judgment upon humankind.

Thesis: God will have the final word on the day of judgment.

Purpose:
- Major Objective: Doctrinal
- Specific Objective: Through the power of the Holy Spirit, I hope to lead each of us in being ready for God's judgment.

Introduction

Outline
   I. God's Judgment Is Not in the World or Personal Events—Luke 13:1-5
  II. God's Judgment Is Not in the "Left Behind" Theology—Luke 17:20-37
 III. God's Judgment Is at the End of Time—2 Corinthians 5:6-10; Revelation 20:12

Conclusion

THE WORD OF THE LORD

Psalm 62:11-12
"One thing God has spoken, two things have I heard: that you, O God, are strong, and that you, O Lord, are loving. Surely you will reward each person according to what he has done."

Matthew 16:27
"For the Son of Man is going to come in his Father's glory with his angels, and then he will reward each person according to what he has done."

2 Corinthians 5:10
"For we must all appear before the judgment seat of Christ, that each one may receive what is due him for the things done while in the body, whether good or bad."

Revelation 20:11-15
> Then I saw a great white throne and him who was seated on it. Earth and sky fled from his presence, and there was no place for them. And I saw the dead, great and small, standing before the throne, and books were opened. Another book was opened, which is the book of life. The dead were judged according to what they had done as recorded in the books. The sea gave up the dead that were in it, and death and Hades gave up the dead that were in them, and each person was judged according to what he had done. Then death and Hades were thrown into the lake of fire. The lake of fire is the second death. If anyone's name was not found written in the book of life, he was thrown into the lake of fire.

INTRODUCTION

This past week I was talking with a gentleman who does not attend our services but listens to some of the sermons on the Web. I asked him which sermons he had listened to, and he had only listened to the negative ones, and he was a little bit upset last week. I encouraged him to give me at least an honest chance and listen to the positive as well as the negative.

I believe Matthew Fox really had something going years ago when he said it is important to travel four paths. The first is the path of "Via Positiva," which is to begin looking at the positive, but if we stay there we become Pollyannas and look through rose-colored glasses. He said it is needful that we also travel the "Via Negativa" road, which means we look with critical eyes and look at the negatives of what is wrong with us, the country, or anything else. But if we stay on that path, we become pessimistic and depressed, so we need to leave that path and also travel a third path, which is "Via Creativa," in which we take the positive and the negative and struggle to create something new, exciting, and different. But if we stay there, we will burn out our creative juices. We need to move on the fourth path, which is the path of "Via Transformativa," which means we then transform it and implement it.[1] And I really believe those four paths are crucial to look at and walk.

I. God's Judgment Is Not in the World or Personal Events—Luke 13:1-5

I reversed that a little bit this morning in the sermon because I want to say two things about God's judgment that I do not believe, and then I will go to what I believe in the last point.

I take seriously God's judgment. But I do not take it as some people do. A decade ago, immediately after 9/11, one of the most well-known preachers in America got on national TV and said America has just been judged. He said 9/11 was God's judgment upon us, and then he named some names and some actions and behaviors that God had judged us for. It was so outrageous that the president of the United States, George W. Bush, called him personally and asked him to recant, and he did within twenty-four hours. Don't you ever believe that he ceased to believe what he said, and don't you ever believe he ceased to preach it. He kept preaching it, just not on national news.

When Haiti was almost destroyed by an earthquake, another of our most popular religious leaders went on national television and said that God had just judged Haiti for a two-hundred-year-old pact with the devil. He said now God was bringing judgment upon us. Just as late as a few weeks ago, Michelle Bachman said on national television that the earthquake near Washington D.C. and up the East Coast and Irene were

God's judgments on Washington; Washington better listen. The country was outraged, and within hours she recanted. We need to seriously think that through on a national level and on a personal level.

How many people that come to my clinical practice believe that God has judged them with their depression? God has judged them with their mental illness. God has judged them with their recent diagnosis of cancer. God has judged them, and on and on it goes. God does not. He did not judge this country on 9/11 and did not judge Haiti, India, or any of the other places. God does not judge us by giving us diseases and tragedies. If that is true, then Jesus Christ's coming and death was a waste. What is the message of Jesus Christ? The message of Jesus Christ is, "I have borne your sins. I have carried your judgment. All of those are placed upon me." And if that is not true, then He came in vain.

And if that is true, God is not running around judging us with earthquakes, terrorist attacks, heart attacks, disease, depression; they don't fit together folks. You can't have them both. You can't have God judging us with world events and personal illness and God's Son, who came to live and love among us and take upon our sins and mistakes. You cannot have them both. They don't fit. So you make up your mind which one you want. I have made up my mind. But you can't have them both. You can't have it both ways. You are going to have to make a choice. But we don't think any of these things through. We don't give them a second thought. Do you know why we do that? We do that out of our insecurities, and we do that out of a failure to understand Israel's history.

Israel's prophets preached that all the time. We have been carried into Babylon because of our sin. We have been attacked, conquered, killed, slaughtered because of our sin. The prophets kept saying wake up, wake up, wake up. But when did that take place? All of that took place prior to Jesus's coming. They didn't have Jesus. They didn't have God's Son, who came and said, "I love you so much that I have come to bear your sins on my sinless body." They didn't have that. We can't preach the Old Testament—God is going to get you, and God is watching you—and preach Jesus's grace and mercy at the same time. It doesn't fit. It won't work. You chose which one you want. If you want to live under God's judgment and be walking around looking to see when He is going to get you, you go right ahead. I am not living that way. I don't live that way. I thoroughly treasure, relish, and enjoy the grace of my precious Lord and Savior. God's judgment does not come upon world events and upon personal disease.

One little real quick story. The first Thanksgiving after I lost the sight in my right eye five years ago, we were celebrating with our black friends at the community building. One of the precious men there (he is too sick to be there with us now) was told that I had just lost my right eye, and he said, "God did that to you, and God is going to bless you so you will be asking Him to take the other eye." I don't think so. I hope He don't take that other eye. I understand that theology. I understand where the man was coming from. I just don't believe it and will never believe it. God does not judge us. The judgment was on Jesus Christ the Son or else His coming and His death are a farce. They are absolutely useless if it is not true.

II. God's Judgment Is Not in the "Left Behind" Theology—Luke 17:20-37

Secondly—and I know some of you are going to really not like this. I kept quiet. I said nothing about it from the pulpit and had a few personal conversations. In the midst of the "Left Behind" series, I remained quiet, but I will not today. God's judgment does not come according to the "Left Behind" series.

Not having grown up in a church, I didn't experience this until my first church. I had this evangelist come in and do a revival for us, and he played the movie *Like a Thief in the Night*. How many of you have seen that? What happened to you? I thought everybody had seen that. It was a time of the late great Planet Earth, and they showed, *The Thief in the Night*, and my youth were scared spitless. All of them ran to the aisle, not wanting to get left. Well, this "Left Behind" and this kind of strategy that is laid out in the "Left Behind" theology is new theology. It didn't come into existence until 1930, created by John Darby. Prior to that, all of this premillennium-postmillennium stuff was not heard of. John Darby brought all of this into focus, followed by Scoffield and a lot of the others.

But quickly let me recap the movie. There was a time in the early 1900s when a minister was being entertained for a call. One of the first questions the minister was asked was, "Are you premillennium?" A millennium means a thousand years. Are you prethousand years, or are you postmillennium? And if you said you were an amillenniest, no thousand years, they didn't talk to you anymore. That was over with. You were too liberal to talk to. I personally am a panmillenniest. I believe it is going to pan out in the end. But if you were premillenniem, what happened was that the rapture took place. *Boom.* You had seen these signs. The rapture comes, and this car will be without a driver. I see some of them now that drive like they are without drivers. The rapture is going to come. *Boom!* And then there will be seven years of horrendous persecution. The Christian people will be taken out. Those left have the mark of the beast on them, and they are going to suffer horribly for seven years. At the end of those seven years, this awesome battle of Armageddon will take place, and Jesus Christ will come in all His glory, and history as we know it will be over with. That is if you are premillennium.

If you are postmillenniem, then the thousand years comes first. There will be a thousand-year reign of peace, and at the end of that, Jesus will come in all of His glory. The rapture, seven years of tribulation, Jesus comes, thousand-year reign of peace, and history is concluded. Postmillenniests believed there would be a thousand years of peace, Jesus comes, history is over.

If you are an amillenniest, there is no thousand years, at least not literally. Panmillenniests just believe it was going to pan out. The problem with all of this is that if you take the rapture, then Jesus comes and the graves give up their dead. If you are alive, Jesus comes for you, and you are gone. And then at the end of a thousand years, Jesus comes again. There is no place in the scripture where it talks about Jesus coming twice. None. Not one. The word *rapture* is not in the Bible. Not one time. Not one.

John Darby started a process where people went to seed over the books of Revelation, Ezekiel, and Daniel. These three books are all Apocrypha books, meaning they were written in hidden language because they were in the midst of trials and all kinds of problems. That is when John's book was written, on the Isle of Patmos when his world as he knew it was falling apart.

Daniel, Ezekiel, Revelation—all of them were written under severe persecution. And we take those books, and we go to seed with them. When I was in the mental health department on Bull Street, when a person came to me and said, "Chaplain, can you get me a Bible?" I had two questions. The first was, "Are you going to take the leaves out and roll a cigarette," because they did that a lot. If they said no, I would say, "Okay, are you going to read Revelation?" And if they said no, then I would get them a Bible. But 80 percent of the people who wanted a Bible wanted to either smoke it or read Revelation. So most of the people did not get Bibles from the chaplain.

I do not believe the "Left Behind" theology is biblical at all. It is human created, and it is human outlined. You cannot find those steps outlined in scripture—in Ezekiel, Daniel, or Revelation. You have to pull them all together to come out with this marvelous kind of scheme if you want to believe it.

III. God's Judgment Is at the End of Time—2 Corinthians 5:6-10; Revelation 20:12

What does God's judgment mean? Well, in my understanding, the scriptures tell us, just like in Corinthians, that we shall all appear before the judgment seat of Christ so that we may receive what is due to us for the things we did when while in the body. God's judgment on us has nothing to do with our salvation. Our salvation is in Jesus Christ and in the mercy, in the grace of Jesus Christ. Our judgment from God is in the last day, and our judgment from God is, "Son, what have you done with the gifts that I gave you, with the mind that I gave you, with the talents and the abilities that I gave you, and with the opportunities that I presented you? Let's talk about how you used these. Let's talk about what you did with what you had."

How many parables did Jesus tell about using your talents? Don't hide them under a bushel. Don't bury them in the ground. How many times? Without question, Billy Graham will go down as one of the greatest evangelists this nation has ever known. Without doubt. But it just may be when it comes to God's judgment and rewards that a little old unknown widow in Podunk Holler may receive a greater reward because she may well have used every ounce of the ability, time, talent, and opportunity she had.

Jesus was seated in a temple one day, and their collection plate was not a little basket like we take around. It was a big round brass trumpet that had a swirl that went all the way to the bottom, and the wealthy would come, drop their coins, and I suspect look around to see how many folks were watching and looking. And one day a little old widow came in, and she dropped a half a penny, a half a penny, and Jesus said, "I want to say to you she gave more than all the rest because she didn't give out of her abundance. She gave out of her need. She gave all she had."

There is God's judgment. And God's judgment is reserved for the last day. Not in this life. The last day. Because you see as you look out on this beautiful lake, if you drop a rock in the lake, ripples go to both sides, and the rock thrown in that lake will not be finished until the last ripple reaches both shorelines. Our lives thrown into the pool of life cannot be fully registered until the very last day of history as we know it. Until the last ripple has reached the other side.

CONCLUSION

Because it is personal, I will share a positive story. I could share some negative ones, but I don't need to do that. A couple of years ago I was shopping in the grocery section at Walmart, and I noticed a young woman looking at me. She had a little baby in the shopping cart and two little babies holding her hands. I spoke, and as I went down the next aisle, I happened to notice her peeping around the corner at the end of the aisle. I wondered what that was about, and I walked down another aisle, and she turned and came down that aisle. She got about five feet from me, and she stopped. Tears welled up in her eyes, and she said, "Are you Gene Rollins?"

And I wanted to say, "No. I don't know him. Never heard of him." But the first thought I had was, *Dear God, I have hurt this person.* That is my own baggage. You know, when the principal used to call my name, I would say, "Oh my God." I never had the thought that he was going to come in there and give me some kind of medal or some kind of reward. No, I knew what he was going to do, and it usually never failed. My expectations were most often fulfilled.

So I look into her tearful eyes, and she gave me her name. "You remember me?" she asked. I said, "No, ma'am. I'm sorry. I don't." And she said, "I was a youth in your church in Greenville. You baptized me when I was eleven years old." I had baptized more than a thousand people. I couldn't remember. She said, "I went on to finish Furman. Then I did a master's in religious education, and I married a minister, and we are pastors of a little church out in Gaston." She said, "I thought that was you, and I just wanted to stop and say thank you for all you meant to me back then."

Well, I started crying. But you see, that is the way it is going to happen. How many lives is she going to touch positively or negatively, and how many lives are they going to touch positively or negatively? It is not going to be over, folks, until the last day. When the last ripple has touched the shoreline of eternity, therein lies God's judgment. Let us pray.

Lord, thank You for the mercies You have extended to us in Jesus the Christ. We confess that we do not deserve, merit, or even expect the kind of mercies and grace that You lavish upon us. For those grace and mercies we give You thanks. Help us to be ready for Your judgment. Help us to prepare for Your judgment. Many parables from Your Word tell us about preparation. And help us in the meantime, as You have extended grace to us, help us to simply be extenders of that grace to others. May it be so, in Jesus's name. Amen.

NOTES

1. Matthew Fox. *Creation Spirituality* (New York: Harper San Francisco, 1991), 17-26.

THOUGHT PROVOKERS

I do not take literally the disproportionate penalty of hell. For example, a killer like Hitler who murdered thousands goes to hell, and a good person who is not a Christian goes to the same hell. Does that seem just or fair?

> "Just as Moses lifted up the snake in the wilderness, so the Son of Man must be lifted up, that everyone who believes may have eternal life in him."

> For God so loved the world that he gave his one and only Son, that whoever believes in him shall not perish but have eternal life. For God did not send his Son into the world to condemn the world, but to save the world through him. Whoever believes in him is not condemned, but whoever does not believe stands condemned already because they have not believed in the name of God's one and only Son. (John 3:14-18 NIV)

CHAPTER 16

I Do Not Take Literally the Bible's Burning Hell

Sermon Syllabus

Text: Matthew 18:1-9

CIT: Jesus used the term *hell* as a metaphor, as he did with cutting off your hand or foot.

Thesis: Hell is a metaphor for separation from God in one's final state of being.

Purpose:
- Major Objective: Doctrinal
- Specific Objective: Through the power of the Holy Spirit, I hope to lead each of us in being committed to God for eternity.

Introduction

Outline:
   I.   The Old Testament Has No Burning Hell—(*Sheol* = Place of the Dead, Mentioned Thirty-One Times)
   II. The New Testament *Hades* (Mentioned Ten Times) is Equal to the Hebrew *Sheol*
   III. The New Testament *Gehenna* (Mentioned Twelve Times) is Jesus's Most-Used Word—Matt. 18:8-9
   IV. The Origin of a Burning Hell—Matt. 18:9
   V. Hell Is Separation from God—Matt. 18:8

Conclusion

INTRODUCTION

If you look to your bulletin, we have for your convenience this passage in Matthew. Before I read the passage and get us into today's subject, I would like to lift up three questions or three meditations that I encourage you to be thinking about in the back of your mind throughout this morning's worship.

So I need to divide you up. If this side, say from Gene on, if you would be thinking about if there is a burning hell, what is it that burns? The body is given to the Earth, and it decomposes, or it is burned or buried at sea. The soul is nonmaterial. The spirit is nonmaterial. So what is it that burns? You all be thinking about that.

The group in the middle be thinking about what could be called a disproportionate penalty. Suppose we have many laws in the land, and one penalty, which is life in prison. If you steal a $25 CD from Walmart, you get life in prison. If you kill ten people, you get life in prison. The person who kills ten people goes to hell. The person, no matter how good or morally ethical they are and how much they love and believe God, if they don't believe Jesus, they go to the same hell. Think about that.

These over on my right, you get the easiest question. First Peter tells us that after Jesus resurrected, He went to hell. We even say in the Apostles' Creed that He descended into hell. The scripture says He went to hell and preached three days. Well, the question is why didn't He burn if there is a burning hell. So let these three questions meander around in your mind as we go through this morning.

The Word of the Lord

Matthew 18:1-9

> At that time the disciples came to Jesus and asked, "Who is the greatest in the kingdom of heaven?"
>
> He called a little child and had him stand among them. And he said: "I tell you the truth, unless you change and become like little children, you will never enter the kingdom of heaven. Therefore, whoever humbles himself like this child is the greatest in the kingdom of heaven.
>
> "And whoever welcomes a little child like this in my name welcomes me. But if anyone causes one of these little ones who believe in me to sin, it would be better for him to have a large millstone hung around his neck and to be drowned in the depths of the sea.
>
> "Woe to the world because of the things that cause people to sin! Such things must come, but woe to the man through whom they come! If your hand or your foot causes you to sin, cut it off and throw it away. It is better for you to enter life maimed or crippled than to have two hands or two feet and be thrown into eternal fire. And if your eye causes you to sin, gouge it out and throw it away. It is better for you to enter life with one eye than to have two eyes and be thrown into the fire of hell.

Not long ago, just after these series were made public in the newspaper, a person confronted me rather aggressively about me not believing in hell. I tried to correct him, though I believe he was one of those who are uncorrectable. I said to him, "I have not put that in print." He said, "Yeah, you did." I said, "No." I said, "What I have put in print is I do not believe in a literal burning hell. I do believe in hell."

So you can leave here telling as many people as you want that I don't believe in a literal burning hell, but do not leave here and tell anyone that I don't believe in hell. If you do, you will be misquoting me horribly. Let us look at the subject, not of hell itself but of a burning hell.

I. THE OLD TESTAMENT HAS NO BURNING HELL

We find in the Old Testament that there is no such concept of a burning hell. The word that is translated by the King James as hell is *Sheol*, and that word is found thirty-one times in the Old Testament, and it is a word most accurately translated to mean "grave" or "place of the dead." So you find *Sheol*, a grave or place of the dead, many times in the Old Testament, but that is what it was. It was a place of the dead. A place where one went after one laid this body aside. When you examine the Old Testament carefully, it does not have a concept of eternal life. It is not there. The hint is in Job. Job said, "If a man dies, shall he live again?" And he doesn't answer that question. But he lifts up a metaphor. If you cut a tree, then that tree might well sprout. So Job is saying that there is hope after this life that we will see a creator. But in the Old Testament there is no clear teaching of eternal life, heaven, or hell.

II. THE NEW TESTAMENT *HADES* IS EQUAL TO THE HEBREW *SHEOL*

In Jesus's day, there was a great division. The Sadducees on the one hand did not believe in heaven or hell, eternal life, *Sheol*, or in the Greek the New Testament *Hades*, which is equal to the Hebrew *Sheol*. They were religious teachers. On the other hand, there was a set of religious teachers called the Pharisees who believed in eternal life, heaven, and hell, and these two groups disputed all of the time.

It was the Sadducees who tried to trap Jesus and said if a man marries a woman and they produce no children and he dies, it is Hebrew law that his brother has to marry his widowed brother's wife and produce children by her. That was the law. Suppose that brother marries her, and he dies with no children, and the next brother marries her, he dies, and you go all the way to seven. Jesus laughed and said, "Surely you know better than this." There is no such thing as marriage in heaven. They were trying to trick him. So what I am saying is in the Old Testament there is no concept of eternal life. There was not a concept of soul until 586 BC when Israel was captured and carried into Babylon, and much of their theology was hammered out in that captivity. They returned to Israel then with a deep sense of soul. So it is just not in the Old Testament.

III. THE NEW TESTAMENT *GEHENNA* IS JESUS'S MOST-USED WORD—MATT.18:8

In the New Testament, the word *Hades*—which is, I think I have indicated, found ten times—is equal to the word *Sheol* in the Old Testament, which means "grave." Jesus used that word a few times, but the word Jesus used the most was *Gehenna*, and it comes from a Hebrew word *Gehenan*, which was a location. It was a valley just east of Jerusalem. In the Old Testament days, it was in that valley that the god Baal and the god Molech had a brass statue that they would build a fire around, and the people would come and offer their firstborn children. Those children would be placed in the arms of Baal and burned to death. That was their greatest sacrifice. That took place in the Valley of Gehenna, and that valley became abhorred by Israel.

Then one other tragedy was added to that. It is recorded in the book of Chronicles that King Ahas of Israel had his three sons slain in that valley. Israel then had a deep, deep dislike, and the valley became their city dump. Within the Valley of Gehenna, they dumped their trash, they dumped their dead animals, they dumped their garbage and their refuse; it was their cesspool. And Jesus said of this place that the worm never dies, and the smoke never ceases to come up, and the fire never ceases to burn. And when Jesus said something about hell, just like in our passage, that is the term He used: *Gehenna*. And when he used that term, it would of course immediately conjure into everyone's mind this horrible stinking place outside their city. That was their city dump. With all of the horrendous history hooked to that place, connected to it, and now it was being used as a place for refuse. Everything you didn't want was dumped there. I don't know of a more graphic metaphor Jesus could have used for hell than this word *Gehenna* and this place of Gehenna.

In our text, Jesus is talking about the greatest in the kingdom, and he says they are little children who are honest, trustful, and faithful, and we must become honest, trustful, and faithful. Then he says if anyone harmed these children, they are going to suffer. And then he says if your hand offends you, cut it off. If your eye offends you, pluck it out. Now, you know that Jesus was not being literal. You know that.

In my days with the State Mental Health Department, I worked with a patient over an extensive period of time who had taken these words literally and gouged his right eye out with a kitchen fork because he had looked upon a woman with lust. I worked for months, trying to help him understand a different metaphorical appreciation for that text. I was never successful. You know that Jesus does not want us to lop off our hands if they in some way sin. Or gouge out our eye if we are lustfully looking. You know that. You know immediately that this is a passage you take interpretively, metaphorically. Well, it is in that context that Jesus uses the same metaphor. Gehenna, a burning hell, is a metaphor. It is a metaphor of horrible separation from God.

Question number one: what is it that burns if we go to hell? Our office manager picked out this graphic picture and put it in the bulletin and asked me if that was okay. I said sure. When someone dies, we put the body in the ground. We bury it, and it decomposes. Our souls are nonmaterial. Our spirits are nonmaterial. What is it that burns? What is left to burn? The Bible does give one sentence of hint that we are given a glorified body in heaven. But is God going to give us a damnable body to be burned in hell? That is not in the Bible. That doesn't even make sense. So when we die, we go to the ground, we go to ashes—ashes to ashes, dust to dust. So what is it that burns in this burning hell?

The second question: truly would we be a just society if we gave a person life in prison for stealing a $25 CD and gave a person life in prison for killing ten people? What kind of justice is that? Well, if a person who kills people, like Hitler, goes to hell and a person who does not believe in Jesus and does not confess Jesus as Lord and Savior, although he or she may be a wonderful faithful Buddhist or an absolutely devoted Muslim, goes to hell, how fair is that? Are they going to the same hell?

And the third question, which is the easiest one to get out of: if hell is burning, how did Jesus spend three days there?

IV. THE ORIGIN OF A BURNING HELL—MATT. 18:9

Where did this metaphor of hell originate? Well, it makes sense to me. How many of you have ever been burned? I remember when I was in the navy in Wisconsin, trying to play John Wayne in this bar fight. I jumped over a counter after a person and knocked a canister of hot coffee onto my neck. I was wearing a blue wool turtleneck navy sweater. I can tell you what burning feels like. And burning is a pain that does not just happen and then it doesn't hurt anymore. It goes on for what seems forever, does it not? So what pain could a culture come up with that would be more graphic, painful, and awesome than burning? I think that is probably part of the origin of it.

How many of you have ever seen molten lava coming out of a volcano, a picture or for real? I have seen it for real in Costa Rica. I swam in water that was about 102 degrees in this pool that was heated from the volcano up the mountain. I watched the sulfur being spewed out and the red molten lava running down the hill. I can imagine looking at that and saying, "Oh yeah, there has got to be a hell down there." And that was their biblical view, that hell was under the ground. That is where that lava comes from. And this is where we live, and heaven is up there. Their world was three-layered. Ours is not. We know better.

So I think the origin of hell is pretty clear. A burn is awful, and the heat in the Earth, a volcano, what a horrible place to be thrown if you reject God. For me, a burning hell is a metaphor. A metaphor of how horrible hell is going to be. Well, Preacher, what is hell for you? Well, a lot of it is right here, folks. I think church people live in a tunnel. All they see is good, wonderful church-going people. We are not out in the world, dealing with inmates, dealing with all kinds of issues a lawyer's office has to deal with or the issues a therapist's office has to deal with. There is a lot of hell going on right here, folks, and don't ever disbelieve that.

V. HELL IS SEPARATION FROM GOD—MATT. 18:8

But hell for me is separation from God. You think for a moment what it would be like. You have rejected any kind of thought, notion, belief about God all of your life, all your earthly life, and you die and come to the realization that you just didn't go into the ground and everything was over. You now realize your spirit and that you were created by a spirit God and that spirit God created you in love, benevolence, compassion, and care, and you rejected that love, benevolence, compassion, and care all of your earthly life, and now you are looking at it in the fullest presentation, but it is not where you are, and you are not where it is. That is my picture of what hell is. When I realize even in this Earth that I have made a mistake, I take it pretty seriously. But could there be a more horrible mistake? To realize I have lived my entire life thumbing my nose at God and God's grace and mercy, and now when my day of choice is over, I look at it in its fullest purity and in its greatest abundance, and I see what I have rejected all my life, and I see now what I will be without it for all of eternity. For me, that is hell.

CONCLUSION

Calvin and Luther both adhered to a strong view of hell, but Calvin at least was no literalist. He wrote:

> Many persons . . . have entered into ingenious debates about the eternal fire by which the wicked will be tormented after judgment. But we may conclude from many passages of Scripture that It Is a metaphorical expression . . . Let us lay aside the speculations, by which foolish men weary themselves to no purpose, and satisfy ourselves with believing that these forms of speech denote, in a manner suited to our feeble capacity a dreadful torment which no man can now comprehend and no language can express.[1]

Let us pray. Oh Lord, we thank You for Your grace and for Your mercy that is continually presented to us in such great abundance, for Your grace and mercy, for Your spirit that cries out to us continually. Walk in love and compassion with me until literally the day You walk with me. May it be so in Jesus's name. Amen.

NOTES

1. John Calvin, *Institues of the Christian Religion,* trans. Henry Beveridge (Grand Rapids, MI. Wm. B. Eerdmans Publishing Col. 1989), 442.

THOUGHT PROVOKERS

I do not literally believe that Jesus created the church. He was a faithful Jew who was trying to reform Judaism.

> When Jesus came to the region of Caesarea Philippi, he asked his disciples, "Who do people say the Son of Man is?"
>
> They replied, "Some say John the Baptist; others say Elijah; and still others, Jeremiah or one of the prophets."
>
> "But what about you?" he asked. "Who do you say I am?"
>
> Simon Peter answered, "You are the Messiah, the Son of the living God."
>
> Jesus replied, "Blessed are you, Simon son of Jonah, for this was not revealed to you by flesh and blood, but by my Father in heaven. And I tell you that you are Peter, and on this rock I will build my church, and the gates of Hades will not overcome it. I will give you the keys of the kingdom of heaven; whatever you bind on earth will be bound in heaven, and whatever you loose on earth will be loosed in heaven." (Matt. 16:13-19 NIV)

CHAPTER 17

I SERIOUSLY WORSHIP THE GOD OF THE BIBLE, BUT I DO NOT LITERALLY WORSHIP THE BIBLE

SERMON SYLLABUS

Text: Matthew 12:1-14

CIT: Jesus placed human need above the temple, ritual, and the Word of God.

Thesis: We are to place the God of compassion above the church, worship, and the Bible.

Purpose:
- Major Objective: Doctrinal
- Specific Objective: Through the power of the Holy Spirit, I hope to lead us in placing God above everything else in life.

Introduction

Outline:
    I.   Jesus Is Lord Above the Bible—Matthew 12:8
    II. Jesus Is Lord Above the Church—Matthew 12:3-8
    III. Jesus Is Lord Above Ritual—Matthew 12:5-6
    IV. Jesus Is Served through Meeting Human Need—Matthew 12:11-13; Matthew 25:31-46

Conclusion

THE WORD OF THE LORD

Matthew 12:1-14

> At that time Jesus went through the grainfields on the Sabbath. His disciples were hungry and began to pick some heads of grain and eat them. When the Pharisees saw this, they said to him, "Look! Your disciples are doing what is unlawful on the Sabbath."

> He answered, "Haven't you read what David did when he and his companions were hungry? He entered the house of God, and he and his companions ate the consecrated bread—which was not lawful for them to do, but only for the priests. Or haven't you read in the Law that on the Sabbath the priests in the temple desecrate the day and yet are innocent? I tell you that one greater than the temple is here. If you had known what these words mean, 'I desire mercy, not sacrifice,' you would not have condemned the innocent. For the Son of Man is Lord of the Sabbath."

> Going on from that place, he went into their synagogue, and a man with a shriveled hand was there. Looking for a reason to accuse Jesus, they asked him, "Is it lawful to heal on the Sabbath?"

> He said to them, "If any of you has a sheep and it falls into a pit on the Sabbath, will you not take hold of it and lift it out? How much more valuable is a man than a sheep! Therefore it is lawful to do good on the Sabbath."

> Then he said to the man, "Stretch out your hand." So he stretched it out and it was completely restored, just as sound as the other. But the Pharisees went out and plotted how they might kill Jesus.

INTRODUCTION

This summer the theme has been "Taking the Bible Seriously but Not Literally." And this last triumphant text illustrates so very, very clearly that I have been in good company. Jesus took the scriptures seriously, but he did not take them literally. And this text proves that so clearly. I would like to take us back to the Old Testament and lift a caution. Unless I am mistaken, the first commandment in Exodus 20 is thou shalt have no other gods before me. The first commandment is that God is to be supreme. There are no other gods before him, not one. And then the scripture, elaborating on that, says that we are to create no graven image. There is to be no human-made image that we place before our spirit God. God did not write the Bible. Humankind wrote it. Inspired of God? Yes. But this book is a product of humankind, and if we lift anything humankind made above our spirit God, we are breaking the first commandment.

I. Jesus Is Lord Above the Bible—Matthew 12:8

There is a difference between this book and God. And I encounter constantly those whose ultimate allegiance is to this book. Their ultimate commitment is to this book. Not the God of this book but this book. And their ultimate energy goes to defending this book. If this book is truly inspired of God, we don't need to defend it. All we need to do is turn it loose. This book needs no defense. We do need to make a distinction that this book does not capture our God. This book does not tell us all that God is. Human words, and that is what this book is, human words cannot capture the sovereignty of God almighty. And it is just a little bit presumptuous of any humankind to believe that I can capture the essence of God almighty in the web of words that I weave. I believe that is the height of grandiosity.

Paul tells us in the book of Romans that God is revealed to us through nature, and the old philosophical argument here is where there is a watch, there must be a watchmaker. Here is a world; there must be a world maker. Paul says that gives testimony to us. And then he says there is a second crucial witness, and that is our conscience. And our conscience tells us there is something beyond us, that there is a holy other. The conscience of humankind, ever since the dawn of humankind, as fundamental as those drawings are on the cave walls, says that those people saw some holy other beyond themselves.

And then we have this testimony. It is the written acts of God in history, but we do grave injustice not only to this book but also to God when we take it literally and fundamentally and take it even as God. There shall be no gods before Him, including this book. I do not worship this book, and I have given forty-seven years to the proclaiming of it. But I knew very early that I did not worship this book. I worshiped the God of this book. And I have struggled for years between understanding the scriptures interpretively and wrestling with them literally, and I have tried to give you this summer the culmination of forty-seven years of struggle with that. So let's look at what Jesus did in this morning's text.

II. JESUS IS LORD ABOVE THE CHURCH—MATTHEW 12:3-8

Jesus and his companions, the disciples, were itinerant preachers, and they were moving from town to town, and they grew hungry. They walked into the wheat fields. Most of the roads just went through the wheat fields. As they walked into the wheat fields and pulled off a heads of wheat, and they would rub it to get the grains out, then they would blow the chaff off, and then they would eat those grains. The travelers had a little pot like a coffee pot, and sometimes they would put the grains in the water and build a little fire beside the road.

It was fully legal for them to do that. Deuteronomy says you cannot prevent a stranger who passes by your fields from going in and pulling heads of your grain and eating it. The law was that they could not take a sickle and harvest. They could not take a piece of equipment into a neighbor's farm and cut, but they could pull the wheat heads with their hands.

The Pharisees saw them doing this, and they said to Jesus, "Do you not understand that your disciples are breaking the Sabbath law?" What were they doing? Well, they were working because they understood that to walk into that field and pull off a handful of grain was actually reaping. And to rub your hands together was actually threshing and to blow the chaff away was also willowing, so they had just made three acts of harvest, and they had worked on the Sabbath day.

Now this was serious business, folks. You don't think this was serious business? Listen to the fifteenth chapter of Numbers. I am not making this stuff up. This is too good. I couldn't make it up. While the Israelites were in the desert, a man was found gathering wood on the Sabbath day. Those who found him gathering wood brought him to Moses, Aaron, and the whole assembly, and they kept him in custody because it was not clear what should be done to him. Then the Lord said to Moses, "The man must die. The whole assembly must stone him outside the camp." So the assembly took him outside the camp and stoned him to death as the Lord had commanded Moses. That is pretty serious stuff. They catch this man gathering sticks on the Sabbath day, and God says to the leader, Moses, "Take him outside the camp and kill him." And they took him outside the camp and killed him for working on the Sabbath day. That, friends, is taking the scriptures literally.

And so the Pharisees said to Jesus, "Do you know what you are doing? You and your disciples have just committed a capital offense. You have broken the Sabbath laws, and it merits death." Notice what Jesus said to them. In a way, he said to them, "You don't even know your own scriptures. Are you not aware how, when David was being pursued by Saul, David and his men were so hungry that they went into the temple and . . . Let me give you just a thumb sketch of the history there.

Priests took seven loaves of bread baked every Saturday, Sabbath day—or baked on Friday—and exchanged them on the Sabbath. They put seven new loaves of bread on the altar. The seven old loaves of bread were taken out and eaten by the priests, and they did that week after week after week. Well, David and his men went into the temple and took the bread and ate it, which was absolutely against the law. Only the priests ate bread that had been consecrated.

And Jesus said, "Do you not know that story?" And then he told them another story. He said, "Who is it that prepares all the burnt offerings on the Sabbath day? Who kills all the animals? Who burns all the animals on the altar? Who separates the meat and gives part of it to you and part of it to the people. Who does all this? Is it not the priests? Are they not working on the Sabbath day?

You know, I have always wondered about that. We preachers get up and preach on not working on Sunday, and who in the world is working the hardest? Just doesn't quite make sense, does it? There is not another day that I work as hard as I do on Sunday. Sunday is the only day I ever go home and take a nap. I can see ten clients in Columbia and drive an hour and drive back an hour and not be as tired as I am at 1:00 p.m. on Sunday. It is having to deal with the likes of you people. No, it is just doing what it is I do.

Jesus said, "You don't know that story? What is wrong with you, people?" And then he made this astonishing statement. Listen: "I tell you that one greater than the temple is here." Wow! Jesus just elevated himself above the teachings of the church and the temple and said, "I will have you to know that there is one in your midst who is greater. Superior over the church, the temple." And then he said these words. Listen again. Verse 8 says, "For the son of man is Lord of the Sabbath." What had he just done? He just said, "You are looking at one that is not only Lord over the temple, Lord over the church, but I am Lord over the scriptures as well." Jesus in no way took the scriptures literally. He took them seriously. And he interpreted and applied them in his life in such a way that they were workable, pragmatic, and life giving. When we make them literal, they can often kill us.

III. JESUS IS LORD ABOVE RITUAL—MATTHEW 12:5-6

There is a story in 1 Maccabee, chapter 2, and for the non-Catholics among us, there are books in the Catholic Bible that take place between the Old Testament and the New Testament, that four-hundred-year interbiblical period. And one of the books in the Catholic Bible is 1 and 2 Maccabee, and we would do good to read that. In 1 Maccabee, a Roman emperor sends out a garrison of men to a bunch of rebellious Jews who are hiding in the caves outside Jerusalem. And Antictus says to this garrison of men, "Wait until dawn of the Sabbath to go get them." Why? Because Antictus knew they would not lift one finger in their defense. And that garrison of Roman soldiers rode into those caves and slaughtered more than a thousand Jews—men, women, and children—and the Jews all stood there with their hands in their pockets, pleading obedience to the law of the Sabbath.

Now you may believe what you believe, but I do not believe God was pleased with that at all any more than I believe God would be pleased if someone came into my house on Sunday afternoon to do harm to me and I said, "It is the Sabbath day, and I cannot do any kind of defense or work." I don't believe God was happy with that kind of obedience at all. And if we ever have an orthodox Jew become president of the United States, somebody better ask him if he will take up arms on the Sabbath day, because Jewish history says he will not. And that entire one thousand men, women, and children were slaughtered because they would not lift a finger to defend their families or themselves because it was the Sabbath day.

Pompeii knew that. In those days, when they would mount attacks on a city of Jerusalem, a walled city, the opposing army would construct a huge mound of dirt outside the city so they could put on top of that mound an observation post. From that post, the commander and chief of the battle could order the army and the strategy and the tactical movements. Pompeii ordered that mound to be built on the Sabbath day only. He knew the Jews would not fire one arrow or make one opposition to their work on their observational mound as long as it was the Sabbath day. And when the mound was finished, from the top of that mound, Pompeii ordered the attack of Jerusalem, and the city was destroyed. The walls tumbled, and the temple burned.

Do I believe God is pleased with that kind of literal obedience? I do not. And it is indicative to me in this scripture that Jesus is not. In this text, Jesus responded three times to human need. His men were hungry, and He took them into the fields on the Sabbath day. He referred His critics to the Old Testament story of David taking his men into the temple and eating the bread to meet human need. And then to press this point further, He went into the temple, and there was a man with a withered hand, and they asked Him if it was lawful to heal on the Sabbath day. They knew the answer to that question. The scriptures condemn it. That is work! One could not work on the Sabbath day. And Jesus said, "You have a sheep, and the sheep falls in a hole, and it is the Sabbath day. Do you not get him out?" They knew the answer to that. They could do that out of mercy. And Jesus said, "How much more valuable is a man, a human being, than a sheep in a pit? What is wrong with you, people?" And He said to the man, "Stretch forth your hand." And he stretched his hand, and it was healed just like the other one. Did Jesus break the Sabbath law? Absolutely. Did He interpret it literally? Absolutely not. He said, "You are looking at the Lord of the Sabbath."

In Mark's Gospel, Mark says the Sabbath was not made for the Sabbath. The Sabbath was made for man. The scriptures were not given to us to lock us up. They were given to us to free us and to set us free. Not to bind us. The very word *religion* itself means to bind up and make whole, and when your religion is not making you whole, it is fragmenting your life, and something is wrong with it. I don't care what its name is.

IV. Jesus Is Served through Meeting Human Need—Matthew 12:11-13; Matthew 25:31-46

Now I want you to see the absolute ludicrousness of literalism. They are accusing Jesus of just breaking the third commandment: honor the Sabbath day and keep it holy. And because He broke the third commandment, listen to what they are willing to do in verse 14.

The Pharisees went out and plotted how they might kill Jesus. Okay, buddy, you break number three, and we will break number five, which says thou shalt not kill. How much sense does that make? None. These scriptures are to be taken seriously, not literally. And to take them seriously constantly does what Jesus did, and that points us not to ritual but to mercy. Not to literalism but the meeting of human need. When we lose sight of that, we lose sight of the God of compassion who called us. Jesus said, "I took them into the grain fields out of compassion for human need; David took his men into the temple out of compassion for human need; I healed the shriveled hand out of compassion for human need. Do you not know that I have hollered all the way through the Old Testament, 'I want mercy not sacrifice!'"

Conclusion

The poet Whittier put it this way:

> O brother man, fold thy heart upon thy brother; Where pity dwells, the peace of God is there. To worship rightly is to love each other, Each smile a hymn, each kindly deed a prayer.

> For in whom Jesus loved has truly spoken—The holier worship which He designs to bless Restores the lost, and binds the spirit broken, And feeds the widow and the fatherless."

> Follow with reverent steps the great example Of Him whose holy work was doing good; So shall the wide earth seem our Father's temple, Each loving life a psalm of gratitude.[1]

It is with great joy at the conclusion of every summer that our elders sit down with me, and we look at what you have given, and we search in our community to find the greatest need, and we distribute what you have given throughout the summer to help meet that need. May this congregation always keep their eyes upon meeting the needs of our brothers and sisters before any and everything else. Let us pray.

Lord, we thank You for this marvelous story out of Your earthly life. We thank You for Your understanding in application of scripture, Your reverence for it but yet Your unwillingness to be legally bound. You were bound by one thing, and that was compassion for Your created humankind. Help us to have that same compassion. In Jesus's name, amen.

Notes

1. William Barclay, *The Gospel of Matthew*, vol. 2 (Philadelphia: Westminster Press, 1957), 28.

CONCLUSION

The seventeen "thought provokers" could be used for a seventeen week Bible study group focusing on this question: if these scriptures are not to be taken literally, how can they be interpreted in a serious, respectful, and reverent way?

1. **I do not take literally the law that says we should kill all homosexuals.** (Lev. 20:13)
2. **I do not take literally the law that says people who commit adultery should be stoned to death.** (Deut. 22:22)
3. **I do not take literally the law that says a child born out of wedlock cannot worship in a congregation.** (Deut. 23:2)
4. **I do not take Jesus's words literally when he said if your eye looks upon another lustfully, you should gouge it out and throw it away.** (Matt. 5:27-30)
5. **I do not take literally the Bible's worldview that the Earth is flat with four corners.** (Rev. 7:1; Luke 16:23; Acts 1:9-11)
6. **I do not literally believe that all of humankind descended from the first couple, Adam and Eve. *Adam* is a transliteration of the Hebrew word *Adom*, which in Hebrew means "men."** (Gen. 2:7, 18-25)
7. **I do not take literally the fact of robbing from God if I do not give 10 percent of my income to the church.** (Mal. 3:8-10)
8. **I do not literally believe that God wills a bird to die or counts the hairs upon my head.** (Matt. 10:29-30)
9. **I do not take literally the law that says a rebellious child should be stoned to death.** (Deut. 21:18-21)
10. **I do not take literally the law that people who worship differently than me should be destroyed.** (Deut. 7:1-6)
11. **I do not take literally that a woman should keep her mouth shut in church.** (1 Cor. 14:33-35)
12. **I do not take literally the law that we should stone to death a bride if she proves not to be a virgin on her wedding night.** (Deut. 22:13-21)

13. **I do not literally believe that a woman who has committed adultery should be killed. Neither did Jesus.** (John 8:1-11)
14. **I do not take the virgin birth of Jesus literally.** (Isa. 7:14; Matt. 1:23)
15. **I do not take literally the law that a person should be put to death if he or she works on the Sabbath (Sunday).** (Exod. 31:12-18) (Num. 15:32-36)
16. **I do not take literally the disproportionate penalty of hell. For example, a killer like Hitler who murdered thousands goes to hell, and a good person who is not a Christian goes to the same hell. Does that seem just or fair?** (John 3:14-18)
17. **I do not literally believe that Jesus created the church. He was a faithful Jew who was trying to reform Judaism.** (Matt. 16:13-19)

SELECTED BIBLIOGRAPHY

Armstrong, Karen. *The Great Transformation*. New York: Alfred A. Knopf, 2006.

Close, Henry T. *Reasons for Our Faith*. Richmond: John Knox Press, 1962.

Harris, Sam. *Letter to a Christian Nation*. New York: Vintage Books, 2006.

Johnson, Timothy. *Finding God in the Questions*. Downers Grove, IL. Inter Varsity Press, 2004.

McGarth, Alister E. *Surprised by Meaning*. Louisville: Westminster John Knox Press, 2011.

Paine, Thomas. *The Age of Reason*. First Part Published 1-28-1794—Second part published 10-25-1795

Phillips, J.B. *Your God is too Small*. New York: The Macmillan Co., 1961.

Robinson, John A.T., *Honest to God*. Philadelphia: The Westminster Press, 1963.

Sire, James W. *Why Good Arguments Often Fail*. Downers Grove, IL: IUP Books, 2006.

Sullivan, Clayton. *Rescuing Jesus from the Christians*. Harrisburg, PA: Trinity Press International, 2002.

Harris, Sam. *The End of Faith*. New York: WW Norton & Company, 2004.

Criswell, W.A., *Why I Preach that the Bible is Literally True*. Nashville: Broadman Press, 1969.

Downing, Crystal L. *How Postmodernism Serves (My) Faith*. Downers Grove, IL: IUP Academic, 2006.

Henry, Carl F. H. *God, Revelation and Authority*. Vol. IV. Waco, TX: Word Books, 1979.

Hitchens, Christopher. *God is not Great*. New York: Twelve, 2007.

Jones, Preston, ed. *Is Believing in God Good, Bad or Irrelevant*. Downers Grove, IL: IUP Books, 2006.

McLargen, Brian Dl. *A New Kind of Christianity*. New York: Harper One, 2010.

Rozak, Theodore, ed. *Ecopsychology.* San Francisco: Sierra Club Books, 1995.

Smith, Huston. *Beyond the Postmodern Mind.* Wheaton, IL: Quest Books, 2003.

Spong, John Shelby. *Jesus for the Non Religious.* San Francisco: Harper Collins Publishers, 2007.

Thielen, Martin. *What's the Least I can Believe and Still be a Christian.* Louisville, KY: Westminster John Knox Press, 2011.

ABOUT THE AUTHOR

The Rev. Dr. Eugene C. Rollins began on May 15, 1984 as the pastor of Liberty Hill Presbyterian Church and retired on December 25, 2011 after twenty-seven years. This was his fifth church in forty-seven years of pastoring. The five churches experienced an average of 180 percent growth under his leadership. The primary reason has been through creating an attitude of pastoral care of the church and community.

For thirty-eight of the forty-seven years he has been bi-vocational or tri-vocational. He is a state licensed professional counselor and also a licensed suwpervisor of professional counselors. He is the founder and director of Midlands Area Pastoral Counseling Services, Inc., established 1984. He is a certified supervisor with the Association for Clinical Pastoral Education, Inc. and a diplomat with the College of Pastoral Supervision and Psychotherapy, Inc. He holds two South Carolina licenses and nine national certifications.

Why I Take the Bible Seriously but Not Literally is Dr. Rollins fourth book to be published. His first, *Grace Is Not a Blue-Eyed Blonde*, was published in 2008. His second book, *The Masks We Wear*, was published in 2010, and his third book, *The Power of the Spoken Word*, was published in 2011. He also has a workbook, *Taming My Tongue*, that is a study guide to recognizing *The Power of the Spoken Word*.

Check his website for other publications and articles—www.generollins.com

Printed in the United States
By Bookmasters